DISTANCE EDUCATION SYMPOSIUM 3:

POLICY AND ADMINISTRATION

**Selected Papers Presented at
The Third Distance Education Research Symposium**

**The Pennsylvania State University
May 1995**

Edited by

Becky S. Duning and Von V. Pittman

Number 11 in the series   **Research Monographs**

**American Center for the Study of Distance Education
The Pennsylvania State University
403 South Allen Street, Suite 206
University Park, PA 16801-5202**

The American Center for the Study of Distance Education is a collaborative effort of the College of Education and the Division of Continuing and Distance Education.

These papers were presented at the Third Distance Education Research Symposium, which was funded in part by AT&T.

**The American Center for the
Study of Distance Education**
The Pennsylvania State University
403 South Allen Street, Suite 206
University Park, PA 16801-5202

ISBN 1-877780-14-6

Table of Contents

Maintaining the Momentum

I am delighted to welcome readers to ACSDE Research Monograph No. 11, and trust that as you read the following articles, written by the leading North American researchers and thinkers about distance education, you will find much to inspire and inform you.

This monograph, Policy and Administration, is one of a series of four, the others being Instruction, Learners and Learning, and Course Design. Each monograph contains a set of articles that have been developed and edited over the past year, based on papers prepared in May 1995 for the ACSDE's Third Distance Education Research Symposium. Each monograph has been shaped and nurtured by an editor, or pair of editors, and I extend thanks to Becky Duning, Senior Project Coordinator for the Western Joint Purchasing Initiative at the Western Interstate Commission for Higher Education, and Von V. Pittman, Associate Dean in the Division of Continuing Education and adjunct professor of postsecondary and continuing education at the University of Iowa, for editing Policy and Administration.

I have given this preface the title "Maintaining the Momentum." This is because I think it is important for us to remember the precedents for this particular work, to have a sense of where it is leading us, and to appreciate that what is written here is part of an on-going, indeed, historical process.

This process began in 1986 with the founding of *The American Journal of Distance Education (AJDE)*, and the establishment soon after of the American Center for the Study of Distance Education. The basic idea of the Center and purpose of *The Journal* has been to bring people together. In the United States the study of distance education, like its practice, has been highly fragmented, with little sense of community, for example, among persons researching correspondence education, education by broadcasting, and by teleconferencing. At the American Center we have tried to provide a number of vehicles for researchers, practitioners, and students who are willing to look beyond technology, who wish to identify and research the learning, instructional design, evaluation, managerial, and policy questions in distance education.

One of the first of these vehicles was the July 1988, "First American Symposium on Research in Distance Education." This was a meeting of around forty people, most of whom had shown their interest in distance education research by having an article published in *AJDE*. They were all known to the editor of *AJDE*, but not to one another. From that meeting emerged a network of persons having a better understanding of where their piece of the distance education research agenda fitted with what was going on in the rest of the field, as well as having a common sense of what needed to be done. This was the agenda for distance education research, broken down into the themes of administration and organization, learning and learner support, course design and instruction, and theory and policy.

Thirty two papers of the First American Symposium on Research in Distance Education were published in *Contemporary Issues in American Distance Education* (Moore 1990).

Following the success of the First Symposium, ACSDE used the same format in November 1990 to organize a similar event but this time focusing on the need to articulate an agenda for distance education research that was international. The first International Symposium on Distance Education Research was held in Macuto, Venezuela, prior to the 15th World Conference of The International Council for Distance Education. Again there were around fifty participants, but this time they came from a dozen countries. Once again the focus was on the state of the research and the agenda for the years ahead, though this time the question was how colleagues could collaborate internationally, not just nationally. Papers from this Symposium were published in ACSDE Research Monograph No. 5.

The impetus towards international collaboration at the Macuto symposium had one very important consequence for the evolution of distance education as a field of study and research. This was the setting up of an electronic network, known as Distance Education Online Symposium (DEOS), one of the first in distance education. By 1996, DEOS has grown to be a network of more than 4000 participants in some sixty countries.

A Second American Symposium on Research in Distance Education was held in May 1991, bringing together in equal numbers participants from the 1988 meeting with others who had published research in *AJDE* or DEOS during the intervening years. Sixteen states were represented as well as Canada. Participants addressed the themes: What have been the results of research since the First Symposium? What are the questions for further research? A poll of participants resulted in the following "top issues":

- Interaction of learner attributes and instructional methods
- Strategies for introducing innovations in course design/delivery
- Need for and effectiveness of interaction (faculty-student, student-student)
- Faculty/administrator development (Moore et al. 1991)

The papers of this Second Symposium were published as ACSDE Research Monograph Nos. 4, 8, and 9, which are available from ACSDE.

From reading these few notes, I hope it will be apparent why I said that the 1995 Symposium should be seen in its historical context. Context will show us the progress we have made, and point to the directions ahead. Just ten years ago there was no defined field of distance education research, and it has taken just ten years to reach the level of sophistication recorded in the pages of this monograph. Context also helps us understand why we are not better than we are. Our growth has been fast, and uncontrolled, and it is not surprising that some seeds, planted hurriedly and hastily brought to blossom, have not flourished. Context, provided by the papers that record the discussions at previous symposia, should help us recognize the sturdy themes, those that have been reiterated as one set of discussants has given way to another. Since each paper cites the sources of its author's thinking, we would be foolish to pass over the opportunity of identifying the pedigree underlying any question that may now appear to be of interest. These are documents that cry out to be used as a means of providing theoretical underpinning for any new venture.

So now, I invite you to turn to Becky Duning's introduction, and then the papers provided in this, the papers from ACSDE's Third American Symposium on Research in Distance Education. I expect there will be a Fourth Symposium before very long, and that perhaps you will wish to attend. Perhaps you will be able to refer to the themes identified in previous Symposia, and show how your research has advanced that agenda. If so, I will be very happy to see you.

Michael G. Moore

References

Moore M., ed. 1990. *Contemporary Issues in American Distance Education.* Oxford: Pergamon Press.

Moore, M., M. Thompson, P. Dirr, eds. 1991. Report on The Second American Symposium on Research in Distance Education. University Park, PA: The American Center for the Study of Distance Education.

1 Introduction

Becky S. Duning

By invitation of The American Center for the Study of Distance Education, we came from Canada, Mexico, and the United States to join a discussion group on research in policy and administration in distance education. Like the other three discussion groups (course design, learners and learning, and instruction) which formed the Third Research Symposium on Distance Education, the policy and administration group—composed of educators, education administrators, and a consultant to government and education institutions—was charged with the task of defining a future agenda for distance education research for higher education.

The assignment was not easy. Starting with the papers prepared by each member of the discussion group, the first task was to identify how current practices in the area of policy and administration might be improved. Then, by homing in on improvements identified by the group as critically important, a list of priority topics and research strategies was to be developed. The list would become our recommendations for the future distance education research agenda.

Stephen Murgatroyd introduces the monograph with a compelling call for educators to use emerging, process-based tools to measure and enhance quality in distance learning, or risk institutional extinction. The discussion group's other papers proceed from an account of historical denouncements of the academic legitimacy of distance education to concerns about faculty rewards and newer imperatives for multi-institutional partnerships. Analysis of the current role of distance education in nation building and social justice in Mexico, and of its use in Canada for telecommunications-based open learning, underscores the multinational prospects of teaching, learning, and research in distance education. Finally, the monograph closes with Christopher Dede's visionary profile of what lies ahead for distance education, adding urgency and promise to the work of educational administrators and policymakers. As for its flow and clarity, whatever this monograph has achieved is attributable in large part to co-editor Von Pittman, whose fine editorial hand is evident throughout.

Many distance education policymakers and administrators will recognize themselves in the personal saga of University of Chicago President William Rainey Harper in the late nineteenth century as he sought to respond to the educational needs of working adults. His efforts to overcome the reticence of faculty members to support wider access to higher education through distance education, while tireless, were never entirely successful. According to historian Von Pittman, Harper would smile knowingly at the present concerns portrayed by Linda Wolcott, such as the need to revisit the balance between intrinsic and extrinsic rewards to faculty. Nor would Harper be surprised by Shirley Hendrick's account of the struggles encountered when higher education institutions try to build viable distance education partnerships.

Where Harper would find himself on unfamiliar ground is in the company of futurist Christopher Dede. Dede describes powerful new telecommunications tools for distance education that would have been unthinkable in Harper's era. No doubt Harper would, however, readily accept the challenge to define the implications of distance education for on-campus student services. After all, most such services continue to have more in common with the needs of students of Harper's day than with students who will typify higher education in the twenty-first century. And Harper would undoubtedly applaud the work of distance educators and their supporters in Mexico and Canada, whose national commitments to meeting the educational needs of the underserved—regardless of personal circumstances, age, or geographic location—are thoughtfully reported by Alejandro Mungaray, Victor Guerra, Carmen Alvarez-Buylla, and Judy Roberts.

Against this backdrop, the discussion group's thinking evolved in discernible stages over the course of the research symposium. The group found its voice initially by reflecting on why the integration of distance education in teaching and learning is thought to hold such promise for higher education. Stage two of the group's dialogue documented some of the abiding concerns, contemporary concerns, and newer preoccupations of distance education researchers and practitioners. Finally, there emerged the underlying themes and specific topics on which to build a future research agenda to improve practice in higher education distance education policy and administration.

To place the topics proposed for the future research agenda in context, the next section summarizes the group's early considerations, and the patterns and themes that ultimately flowed from the discussion.

Placing the Proposed Research Agenda in Context

The Promise of Distance Education. The group's sense of the importance of integrating distance education into higher education instruction centered on three major considerations. First, the use of distance education to enhance instructional capacities offers faculty an opportunity to reach their full potential. Second, the integration of distance education into traditional instruction gives students, wherever they are located, access to the best educators. Finally, distance education gives higher education a way to respond more effectively to society's demands that postsecondary education institutions make a greater contribution to economic development. Reflecting this expectation, state legislatures are becoming insistent in their calls for higher education to be more accountable for meeting the educational needs of the workforce. Clearly, higher education institutions must become more responsive to society's perceived needs, or other organizations will respond for them.

The group concluded that distance education provides the force to develop new directions in organizational planning and to enhance teaching and learning at all levels. There was agreement that a primary strength of telecommunications is its support for greater learner-centeredness, defined as experiential and interactive education, and its efficacious use of faculty time and other instructional resources. We acknowledged the enormous educational power placed at the fingertips of both faculty and students by telecommunications, and we recognized the many forms of consumer power education can inspire, such as incentives for underserved communities to mobilize for inclusion in the emerging information infrastructure.

Members of the discussion group generally agreed that the integration of distance education into postsecondary education must center on faculty as providers and on students as both consumers and learners. Four critical methods for strengthening the faculty's role in distance teaching and learning were identified: 1) alter the way in which faculty are evaluated; 2) ease faculty into the use of distance education tools and approaches; 3) reconceptualize the means by which the work of educational institutions can be organized to add value to the instructional process; and 4) recognize the barriers that early users of new educational technologies may unintentionally create when others try to catch up (Geoghegan 1994).

Consumer-protection efforts have long shielded students from educational enterprises of questionable repute by denying these ventures the right to compete for business in specified geographic areas. As the public demand for greater access to education has increased, some regulators have begun to consider consumer protection in terms of greater accessibility. Consequently, regulators may ultimately be more inclined to encourage, rather than to limit, competition among education enterprises, and to explore how communities can be encouraged to support learners engaged in distance education.

During the course of the discussion, the group identified abiding concerns, contemporary concerns, and newer preoccupations as appropriate topics for a future research agenda:

Major Abiding Concerns of Distance Education in Higher Education

1. Expectations within the academy that distance education must be self-financing.

2. Scholars' skepticism about the academic legitimacy of teaching and learning in a distance education format.

3. Faculty resistance to distance education policies and practices that do not lead to traditional rewards and advancement in higher education.

4. "Guilt by association" with the claims and practices of questionable commercial distance education enterprises.

Major Contemporary Concerns of Distance Education in Higher Education

- Resource Allocation. Policymakers must work toward greater consensus on the appropriate allocation of national and institutional resources to enhance the availability of distance education at the postsecondary education level.

- Consumer Awareness. Higher education institutions must be more responsive to consumer needs and society's expectations for accessible, affordable, and culturally sensitive education.

- Partnerships. If higher education is to achieve cost efficiencies, strategies are needed for postsecondary education institutions to develop more public/private partnerships in support of distance education.
- Enhance Professional Capacities. Human resource development needs to include the enhancement of faculty capacities to use distance education approaches to teaching and learning.

- Soft Landing. Higher education institutions need to develop practices that can ease faculty into the integration of distance education media in teaching and learning.

Newer Preoccupations of Distance Education in Higher Education. The policy and administration discussion group identified emerging preoccupations that are consistent with the forces acting on higher education, as documented by The Pew Charitable Trusts through individual Campus Roundtables convened over the past two years in partnership with The Pew Higher Education Roundtable. Central to these forces is the expectation that higher education will achieve broader public relevance in the following ways:

- Economic relevance. Act as an engine for the creation of jobs.
- Social relevance. Reinforce cultural identity in the process of teaching and learning.
- Equity. Work toward access to postsecondary education for all.

The Campus Roundtables identified major changes that have influenced how institutions of higher education see themselves (The Pew Higher Education Roundtable 1A-5A). Demographic shifts have altered the size and composition of the workforce and the population of higher education students. Most notably, the numbers of women and adult students have increased substantially, and the growing racial and ethnic heterogeneity of the society is increasingly reflected within higher education. In addition, the growth in the service-sector economy has made a college degree increasingly necessary for workers' earning power over time.

Most importantly, the public is increasingly disenchanted with the perceived outcomes of education at all levels. This attitude has been translated into demands that higher education demonstrate greater and more measurable productivity, at reduced costs. In a related development, a public perception that higher education should be as readily available and convenient as other consumer services has emerged. Finally, the academy has lost its sense of a "framework of shared values in which the process of teaching and learning can occur" (The Pew Higher Education Roundtable 4A). Although the discussion of the research symposium policy and administration group was cast differently than that of the Higher Education Roundtables, there is a shared recognition of the need for higher education institutions to respond to the drumbeat of change.

Themes Underlying the Future Research Agenda

The following critical themes in policy and administration in higher education distance education were identified:

- Structure higher education institutions more effectively to carry out a mission that includes distance education.
- Validate distance education in higher education.
- Designate essential support services.

- Allocate resources more appropriately for distance education.
- Identify and address human development issues associated with distance education.

Proposed Future Research Agenda for Distance Education Policy and Administration

Flowing from these themes, the following areas of study emerged for a future research agenda. Researchers are encouraged to formulate research questions within these areas and are urged to consider the use of cross-cultural research teams in their research designs.

I. Areas for Research Concerned with Faculty

- How do faculty members in postsecondary education institutions view the prospects for their careers in the next decade?
- What are faculty members' expectations and perceptions of the impact of telecommunications-assisted distance education on their role within the academy?
- What are the critical barriers to faculty members' achievement of their professional goals?
- How does the reward structure for higher education faculty diminish or enhance their capacities to teach and conduct research within an environment that includes a commitment by higher education institutions to distance education?
- How are higher education policies for faculty hiring and retirement affected by the increased commitment of postsecondary education institutions to distance education?
- What policies will advance the establishment of organizational structures in higher education institutions to support faculty adoption of instruction based on the media of distance education?
- What competencies are required of faculty who use distance education media for instruction?
- How do public attitudes toward teaching and research affect their relative importance in higher education institutions committed to instruction that includes distance education?

II. Areas for Research Associated with Change in Higher Education

- What are the benefits and penalties of applications of telecommunications to distance education in higher education?
- What is the efficacy of a postsecondary education institution's investment in distance education, and how is it measured?

- How do the costs of telecommunications-assisted teaching and learning vary with the type of application?
- What is the impact of telecommunications-assisted distance education on such campus-based services as housing, food services, library services, and book stores?
- Is there a life cycle for partnerships formed by postsecondary education institutions to advance distance education? .
- How is organizational change within higher education institutions influenced by the addition of telecommunications-assisted distance education to the institutional mission or by partnerships for distance education?
- What organizational models enhance higher education institutions' responsiveness to learners as consumers of services?

III. Areas for Research Associated with Consumer Protection in Higher Education

- How can access to higher education for the underserved be maximized using models to fund and develop an integrated information infrastructure?
- Does differential public access to the information infrastructure influence socioeconomic divisions in society?
- What are learners' perceptions and expectations of distance education in higher education?
- How are higher education residency requirements applied to telecommunications-assisted and other forms of distance education?

Cross-cutting Considerations with Course Design, Learners and Learning, and Instruction

The symposium groups that centered on course design, learners and learning, and instruction identified major areas of mutual concern with policy and administration. All groups shared a sense of urgency for research on the link between institutional governance and course design. Several groups highlighted the value of developing a body of literature on which to base policies in support of faculty and learner satisfaction. Like the policy and administration group, the discussion group on learners and learning acknowledged a critical need for greater understanding of the influence of instructional rewards on the integration of distance education into postsecondary education.

Similarly, the discussion group on instruction advocated study of the organizational culture of teaching and learning and its influence on the instructional outcomes of distance education. As in the discussion group on policy and administration, the discussion group on instruction acknowledged the value of achieving greater understanding of faculty and learner perceptions and expectations of distance education.

Conclusion

Telecommunications applications to teaching and learning in higher education were widely praised during the research symposium. In the words of the participants, "distance education media force faculty and administrators to plan better," "learners can be involved actively as learner/researchers seeking answers to experiential problems," "telecommunications technologies inspire communities to mobilize to get what they want in order to participate in the information infrastructure," and "telecommunications promotes the efficacious use of faculty time." Yet the participants also cautioned that it is imperative to ensure that the humanity of educators, administrators, and policymakers is respected during the introduction of new electronic interactions that appear to hold such promise for educators and learners alike. At the least, a shared research agenda for distance education within higher education will encourage studies that ground conventional wisdom in practical research.

References

Geoghegan, W. H. 1994. *What Ever Happened to Instructional Technology?* Norwalk, CT: BM Academic Consulting.

The Pew Higher Education Roundtable. 1995. Twice imagined. *Policy Perspectives* 6(1):1A-11A.

Becky S. Duning

2 Responding to the Challenge of Quality in Distance Education

Stephen Murgatroyd

Introduction

Quality is an elusive and very confusing construct. It is used as a term of protection and defense as well as a term of praise. It is used to create boundaries and divisions as well as a vehicle for creating teams and integration. It is, in short, a widely misunderstood term. In this paper, quality is defined in terms of "fitness for use" of a program or activity, where value of "use" is determined by students and those who seek to use their competencies for some specific purpose.

In this paper I want to develop some frameworks within which we can understand the construct "quality" as it applies in distance education, and to develop the idea that organizations and programs will require a balance between three types of quality systems: quality assurance, contracted quality, and customer-driven quality (Murgatroyd and Morgan 1993). I also want to suggest that we need to become rigorous about these three kinds of quality and keep them differentiated.

Five Key Concerns

Before exploring these ideas, it is important to begin with five key understandings regarding the debate about quality in education.

1. **Quality has nothing much to do with resources. Instead, it concerns the achievement of competency outcomes by means of**

sustainable and efficient processes. Programs are not better because they cost more or have more modern capital equipment or a higher teacher to student ratio. While there is a perceived equation that more resources equals quality, there is little empirical evidence to support such an assertion. Further, reducing the resource level for activities does not necessarily lead to a diminution of quality either. Indeed, a key argument in favor of distance learning organizations, such as the Open University in Britain and Athabasca University in Canada, is that quality can allow education to be delivered to a larger number of people at a significantly lower cost.

2. **Quality is measurable and not abstract.** It is performance-related quality that we look for in education. Some of the measures—sociability, adaptability, creativity, etc.—may be "softer" than harder measures of specific cognitive abilities. Nevertheless, quality should be concrete. Many educational objectives are expressed in unmeaningfully abstract and unmeasurable terms. A focus on quality requires a degree of concreteness about performance that is most often associated with the use of key performance indicators.

3. When we look at the assets of an organization, **quality is part of a broader category of constructs we use to develop a profile of the symbolic capital of the organization.** Organizations have four kinds of capital: intellectual/pragmatic capital, financial capital, environmental capital, and symbolic capital. The latter relates to reputation, history, and patterns of response to the work of the organization. In small business we call this "good will"; in larger organizations it is called "symbolic capital." Increasingly, in the business environment, we can put a dollar amount on this form of capital. What should be noted here is that quality is only one of numerous components of symbolic capital, and should not be confused with reputations. Since reputation often lags behind current practice, an organization can have a good reputation, but poor quality services and products.

4. **Quality is not fixed in time.** It is a moving target that is directly affected by the actions of competitors. Thus a learning system which we developed and implemented in 1994 using Lotus Notes technology may look very dated when the next major groupware product is released by Microsoft in 1996.

5. **Quality is more often linked to simplicity than complexity.** Just as quality is not necessarily linked to resource levels, so it is not linked to complexity. Some of the most powerful distance learning systems are inexpensive, simple, and have a direct and immediate appeal to students. Quality and technological complexity may in fact have an inverse relationship.

These observations are based on an extensive review of the quality literature (Murgatroyd and Morgan 1993) and drawn from substantial world-wide consulting work in education. They suggest to me that we need to be very clear about the nature of quality at different levels within a distance education program if the construct is to be helpful to us.

Three Kinds of Quality

In this paper, as elsewhere (Murgatroyd and Morgan 1993, 47-56), a distinction is made between three different kinds of quality alluded to earlier: quality assurance, contract conformance, and customer-driven quality.

Quality Assurance. Quality assurance is usually achieved by inspection, formal evaluation processes, and peer review. Most accrediting agencies claim to practice quality assurance in that they apply generalized standards and procedures to examine the provisions for learning within an educational organization. For example, the American Assembly of Collegiate Schools of Business (AACSB) has a set of standards against which organizations seeking accreditation are judged and accredited. These include such aspects of teaching and learning as:

a. freedom of action of the organization;
b. admission standards;
c. qualifications for teaching faculty;
d. deployment of faculty in terms of teaching loads;
e. curriculum balance and specifications;
f. student assessment processes;
g. library resources;
h. facilities for study, including student technologies; and
i. standards maintenance.

The standards permit some local variation, but in many cases prescribe the framework for accreditation. For example, the AACSB standards make assumptions about tenure being the basis of academic employment and that doctoral degrees are a necessary precondition for teaching at the undergraduate level. Yet such standards are not necessarily validated by empirical data, but rather by tradition.

While accreditation is seen as essential for certain purposes such as marketing, attracting faculty, securing grants, or obtaining awards, it is also seen by many as limiting in three distinct ways.

First, quality assurance standards for teaching and learning within such accreditation systems are perceived to "lag behind" developments in new technologies for teaching and learning. Truly innovative schools tend to have to downplay or deny innovation to "meet standards." Second, while the philosophy of accreditation may be open to new ways of thinking—the AACSB standards, for example, state clearly that "departures from Standards will be accepted if the school demonstrates that high quality is achieved"—yet most evaluation teams lack experience of quality-based innovations in distance learning. In short, there is a gap between rhetoric and reality. Third, there is a view that accreditation standards have an implied purpose of protecting the academy against change. That is, setting tough standards in the name of quality has, in fact, restricted market driven competition and innovation and protected the "traditions" of existing education institutions.

As we shall see, quality assurance need not be undertaken from a framework of predetermined standards and quantifiable rules. However, most quality assurance activities within education are still based on peer review, with external "experts" from established organizations reviewing new programs and passing judgments. In Britain, this process was known as "inspection." By contrast, a key tenet of the quality movement is to minimize external inspection, create quality systems which are effective in terms of the mission and goals of the organization, and bypass the terms established via abstract standards usually grounded in another era.

Contract Conformance. A different way of looking at quality is to examine the explicit and implied learning contracts established between an organization and its students and staff, and to determine the extent to which the letter and spirit of these contracts have been met. The contract referred to here is not simply the legal contract an institution has with a learner, normally expressed in terms of deadlines and regulations, but also involves the implied contracts for learning that develop within an organization.

It is normal in distance education to begin each lesson of instruction with learning objectives. In addition, program design is increasingly based on competency commitments outlined to learners at the outset of entering a program. Thus, quality assessment through contract conformance requires the development of systems of quality evaluation which examine in a rigorous and repeated way the extent to which the terms of these contracts are met.

This approach applies as much to operational aspects of learning as to the content of learning. For example, it would be appropriate in this kind of quality examination to look at such things as turnaround time for feedback and evaluation from assessments, the quality of feedback from an examination, the utility of technological usage, and so on.

Customer-Driven Quality. Most systems for quality within educational organizations treat the student as the end-point of the quality system. Program quality is examined in terms of such things as grade point averages of students leaving the course; the scores of students entering a program on standardized admission tests, such as the GMAT; drop-out; rates and completion rates. Rarely is program quality examined in terms determined by the students acting as customers.

Indeed, in some circles there has been a direct rejection of the idea that students are customers. More commonly, professors claim that their real customers are their academic peers and society in general. While there is no denying that communities have a vested interest in the performance of their publicly funded educational institutions, there are direct and specific conditions of customer satisfaction which must be addressed if students' and employers' expectations are to be met. A quality education system rigorously identifies the conditions of customer satisfaction and designs processes to secure delivery of services to meet these conditions.

The Quality Frame. Although many writers such as Sallis (1993) have presented these three kinds of quality frameworks as alternatives, they are not. On the contrary, organizations need to have quality systems for all three forms of quality so as to ensure quality performance. Whereas in the past the emphasis has been on formal quality assurance systems, this will change over time to a stronger emphasis on market-driven quality. Consequently, customer-driven quality and contract conformance will become increasingly important in the delivery of quality education.

Determining the Quality of the Design of a Learning Organization

In looking at quality, it is first necessary to ask some questions about the organization which is delivering a course, program, or set of activities through distance learning. Most major quality research suggests that customers switch from one organization to another with the same or a similar product mainly because of service quality issues as opposed to issues related directly to the product. Being treated badly by a registry official is more likely to lead a student to transfer than does a poor textbook for a course (Whiteley 1991). In fact, 65% of all such "defections" come from operational and service issues, as opposed to product related issues.

The Baldrige Award. How do we determine the quality of the learning organization that is delivering the distance education program, especially given that their "rules of engagement" in the marketplace are often different by design from the "rules of engagement" used by more traditional organizations using more traditional delivery? One way some organizations have assessed the organizational design for quality is to make use of the Malcolm Baldrige Award criteria as the basis for organizational review and assessment. The award was established in 1987 in the United States by Congress as the President of the United States' Quality Award, more commonly known as the Malcolm Baldrige Award (named after a former Secretary of State). It is awarded annually on the basis of a systematic and rigorous examination of the quality practices of applicant organizations. Initially focusing on private sector enterprises, in 1995 eligibility for the award was extended to educational organizations.

The Baldrige criteria for organizational evaluation focuses on the organizational features of quality design. The categories and weightings for the evaluation process presented in Table 1 are accompanied by rigorous procedures to score and evaluate an organization. Each component of this evaluation framework is used to examine the design of the organization in its own terms. That is, the evaluation does not begin with predetermined standards, as in accreditation. Rather, it begins with the vision, mission, and business plan of the organization in order to assess the organization in its own terms. For example, under category 7.1, Knowledge of Customer Requirements and Expectations, the Baldrige examining team are required to look at the following criteria:

a. Processes for identifying market segments, customer and potential customer groups, including customers of competitors, and their requirements and expectations through surveys, interviews and other contacts;

b. Process for identifying product and service quality features and the relative importance of these features to customers and customer groups;

c. Cross comparisons with other key data and information, such as complaints, losses and gains of customers, and performance data that may yield information on customer requirements and expectations and on key product and service features; and

d. How the organization evaluates and improves the effectiveness of processes for determining customer requirements and expectations such as improved surveys, other customer contacts, analysis, and cross comparisons.

There are no prescriptions to how best to achieve the outcome required under each of these terms. Instead, each of these key points is rated using a rigorous rating scale that emphasizes the way the organization has designed its systems and processes to produce outcomes.

It is likely that we will see the development of alternative accreditation systems along these lines, especially as regional monopolies break down and global competition for students grows. Thus, accrediting agencies would be well advised to move away from their approach to quality in terms of standards and towards a process orientation assessment of the design of learning organizations. It would provide greater opportunity for innovative programs to benefit from being subject to quality assurance and contract conformance review. At the same time, this approach permits the development of a systematic understanding of an effective learning organization.

Table 1: The Baldrige Award Categories and Weights

1.0 Leadership		100
Senior Executive Leadership	30	
Quality Values	20	
Management for Quality	30	
Public Responsibility	20	
2.0 Information and Analysis		60
Scope and Management of Quality		
Data and Information	35	
Analysis of Quality Data and Information	25	
3.0 Strategic Quality Planning	90	
Strategic Quality Planning Process	40	
Quality Leadership Indicators in Planning	25	
Quality Priorities	25	
4.0 Human Resource Utilization		150
Human Resource Management	30	
Employee Involvement	40	
Quality Education & Training	40	
Employee Recognition and Performance		
Measurement	20	
Employee Well Being and Morale	20	
5.0 Quality Assurance of Products and Services		150
Design and Introduction	30	
Process and Quality Control	25	
Continuous Improvement	25	
Quality Assessment	15	
Documentation	10	
Business Process Quality	25	
Supplier Quality	20	
6.0 Quality Results		150
Quality of Products and Services	50	
Comparison of Quality Results	35	
Business Processes/Continuous		
Improvement	35	
Supplier Quality Improvement	30	
7.0 Customer Satisfaction		300
Knowledge of Customer Requirements		
and Expectations	50	
Customer Relationship Management	30	
Customer Service Standards	20	
Commitment to Customers	20	
Complaint Resolution for		
Quality Improvement	30	
Customer Satisfaction Determination	50	
Customer Satisfaction Results	50	
Customer Satisfaction Comparisons	50	
TOTAL POSSIBLE SCORE		1000

ISO9000. A second method for assessing the quality of design for a learning organization is to use ISO9000 (BS5750). The International Standards Organization (ISO) is a Geneva-based organization supported by governments as a not-for-profit center for the development of practice and safety standards. Since 1989, both the British Standards Institute and ISO have shown considerable interest in education and have started to apply ISO9000 to educational organizations, especially in further and technical education and increasingly in higher education.

The underlying philosophy of ISO9000 is similar to the Baldrige Award. It is a rigorous system to examine the extent to which organizations have designed quality into all of their processes. While the ISO9000 and Baldrige categories differ, they cover similar ground. Although the costs to securing ISO9000 designation are substantial and the time to implement this standard can be between sixteen and twenty-five months, it is a rigorous approach to the development of quality processes. While both the Baldrige and ISO9000 instruments will require refinements for wider applications to education, these tools are preferable to the use of abstract accreditation standards.

Program Quality

Program quality is the normal domain of accreditation bodies which make extensive use of peer review. The problem is that almost all extant models of quality assurance used by accreditation bodies are based on the following set of prevailing assumptions:

a. The ideal form of teaching is classroom-based, which leads to the perpetuation of related assumptions about teacher to student ratios.

b. The ideal instructor is highly qualified. The more qualified, the better the instructor is assumed to be, although there is no necessary link between academic qualifications and teaching skills. The ideal instructor also holds tenure, which is assumed to be linked to qualifications that provide continuity and quality input.

c. The ideal course can be expressed in terms of hours of instruction versus hours of active learning.

d. Access to appropriate resources, e.g. library resources, computing resources, or laboratory bench resources can be measured by formulas developed by accreditation bodies working in non-virtual teaching environments.

e. Benchmark programs should be used to frame quality issues, and these programs are most appropriately those at large universities with high capital costs and high staff costs.

f. Outcomes are best assessed in terms of grade point average achievement and classification analysis as opposed to competency-based measures.

Underlying these accreditation assumptions and practices is the notion that quality is defined by reference to an idealized model of "best practice," defined in terms of the dominant ideology of teaching. Indeed, contemporary principles of accreditation have more to do with the design of instruction than the process of learning. Peer review also encourages greater focus on instructional design and competencies than on the experience of learning. Few site visits involve sitting in classrooms, working with students, or competency-based outcome evaluation.

Instead, some accrediting bodies have specific ratios and rules which are inflexible, especially those related to staff to student ratios. These are based not on empirical evidence concerning efficacy but on standards agreed and negotiated by vested interests, i.e. professors. Another key area in which accreditors assert control relates to entry qualifications for programs. Since quality outputs are typically viewed by accreditors as a function of quality inputs, the principle of open admission, which is central to the Open University (UK) and Athabasca University (Canada) is grounds for quality rejection by almost all U.S. accreditation agencies.

Most of the considerable body of literature on program evaluation practices begins with assumptions about instructional processes. To ground these assumptions, we need new and powerful learning process evaluation tools for quality assurance, contract conformance, and market-driven quality assessment of programs. In the absence of these evaluation tools, the enhancement of program quality will be constrained by the perilous and problematic practice of peer review.

Benchmarking

One practice which we need to encourage is that of benchmarking that allows comparing program and organizational performance for the same or similar programs across organizations and organizational types. For example, it would be valuable to my team to compare customer and employer satisfaction with MBA programs, along with many other variables, between and across distance education institutions, and more conventional programs around the world.

Our claims to quality and performance are difficult to substantiate in the absence of benchmarking data. One service the International Council on Distance Education could provide to its members would be an international clearinghouse for quality and performance data for distance education. In this way, organizational planners, program designers, and evaluators could benchmark their organizations against others in the same "industry."

Conclusion

Education is a growth industry experiencing major change. Students are more discerning about how and where to invest tuition funds. Employers are more demanding about the quality and performance of educational organizations, so much so that some postsecondary education institutions offer performance competency guarantees to employers of their graduates. Several long-standing organizations associated with distance education are playing an increasingly global role, principally with professional and applied programs.

Regional monopolies for education are breaking down as videoconferencing, computer-managed learning, and multimedia learning systems make artificial geographic boundaries irrelevant. Private sector investment in training and learning systems is growing as numerous companies recognize the competitive advantage that results from a workforce engaged in learning, and through investments in employees' technological competency. In addition, governments, especially in countries where education is publicly funded, are increasingly concerned with educational value, quality assurance, and performance in spite of reductions in overall real expenditure on education.

Educational organizations face massive challenges as these market-related forces unfold. In addition, the globalization of education and the emergence of new technologies will create new entrants into education markets. Customers will become more and more demanding as competition grows within these markets and then costs of education rise. Quality is a key to understanding competitive advantage in postsecondary education. Unless learning organizations dedicate themselves to quality processes and begin to use the kind of quality practices described here, they may be at a competitive disadvantage. Attention to quality will increasingly make a difference not just to performance but to organizational survival.

References

Murgatroyd, S., and C. Morgan. 1993. *Total Quality Management and the School.* London: The Open University Press.

Sallis, E. 1993. *Total Quality Management in Education.* London: Kogan Page.

Whiteley, R. 1991. *The Customer Driven Company - Moving from Talk to Action.* New York: Addison Wesley.

3 Harper's Headaches: Early Policy Issues in Collegiate Correspondence Study

Von Pittman

Introduction

John D. Rockefeller knew immediately who he wanted to head the great university he was founding, the "new" University of Chicago. He spared neither time, effort, nor money to get him. On the other hand his choice, Professor William Rainey Harper, then of Yale University, was tentative. While Harper allowed Rockefeller and the trustees to formally elect him president in September 1890, he insisted upon six months in which to make a final decision. During that period, even as he repeatedly expressed doubts about his desire to accept the position, he began to make plans for the organization of the university and to search for a faculty of the highest distinction (Storr 1966).

Harper began writing a series of six bulletins in which he described the missions, organization, and activities of the new university that would officially open in October 1892. In *Official Bulletin, No. 1,* issued in January 1891, he laid out the basic structure, including Extension as one of five integral divisions of the University. He also began "raiding" the faculties of the most celebrated universities in the United States. In an amazingly short time, the two efforts clashed.

Harper hired the first two "head professors" (akin to department chairs), J. Laurence Laughlin and William G. Hale, both of Cornell, in December 1891, by expending a great deal of effort and Rockefeller's money. Less than six weeks later, Harper faced his first faculty controversy. Laughlin and Hale learned that Harper intended to allow students to do half of their work, at any level, by correspondence study, and went into a snit. They complained that Harper had taken on too much authority and had begun making decisions that should have been left to the faculty. In addition, they demanded that he travel to Cornell to discuss this issue, as well as a number of other matters having to do with faculty governance (Storr 1966).

Harper first tried to paper over the differences between himself and his first two "stars," but he finally agreed to meet with them in Ithaca. In the meantime, however, they had found more to complain about. Harper yielded on a number of matters, including the establishment of a faculty senate. However, he did not give in on the issue of correspondence study. As specified in *Official Bulletin, No. 6* (1892), which detailed the organization of Extension, students would be allowed to take up to half the work required for a graduate or undergraduate degree via correspondence courses.

Harper's Commitment: The Roots of Collegiate Correspondence Study

Long before Harper started organizing the University of Chicago, he had established himself as the country's leading authority on correspondence study. Not only had he essentially defined the format, he had given the medium both credibility and visibility, due to his prominence as an educator. Harper first involved himself in correspondence study during his tenure at the Baptist Union Theological Seminary, at Morgan Park, in Chicago. To fill his summers, he developed intensive ten-week Hebrew courses. In 1881, in response to a demand from pastors and others who wanted to study Hebrew, but who could not come to Chicago, he converted his course to the correspondence format.

According to his Morgan Park colleague Eri Hulbert (1906), Harper read an advertisement that "some rabbi" planned to use the correspondence method to teach Hebrew. Intrigued by the idea, Harper began drawing up lessons for an elementary Hebrew course. He used an electric pen (something like a wood burning tool) to cut stencils, so that he could produce Hebrew characters in "lesson slips," his basic instructional device. The need for better instructional materials resulted in his first seven published works. Not reticent about this enterprise, Harper used denominational yearbooks to build mailing lists of pastors and mailed out what Hulbert called "alluring circulars" (p. 174) promoting the study of Hebrew by mail. Harper incorporated his summer teaching and correspondence courses under the name of the American Institute for Sacred Literature (AISL), which moved with him from Morgan Park to Yale, and back to Chicago.

In 1883, Harper began taking his intensive Hebrew courses to the Chautauqua institutes. He decided to use the correspondence method to follow up on the work of summer students. Chautauqua eventually began using correspondence study extensively, up to the point of granting full degrees through a college program sanctioned by the State of New York. Between the

AISL and Chautauqua, the correspondence teaching format gained a great deal of visibility and popularity in the 1880s. At the request of Bishop John Heyl Vincent (1885), Harper wrote an extended essay codifying the elements of correspondence study, which was included in a book on Chautauqua.

In fact, Harper's initiatives did not represent the first efforts in collegiate correspondence study. Illinois Wesleyan University began offering correspondence programs at both the baccalaureate and graduate levels in 1874. Unrelenting skepticism about the method finally resulted in their termination in 1906 (Gerrity 1976). From all indications, Illinois Wesleyan ran a rigorous program, but some other "innovators" did not. Institutions such as the University of Wooster (Ohio) and the American Temperance University (Tennessee) conferred advanced degrees for *in absentia* study (Portman 1978). For the most part, financial problems had led to the creation of these schools of the sort that Robert Penn Warren characterized as "long on Jesus and short on funds" (1946, 168).

By the time Harper wrote correspondence study into the plans for the University of Chicago, the other extant programs were either dying or discrediting themselves and the instructional method. His decision to champion the method gave it renewed life at the collegiate level. While the University of Chicago would eventually terminate the program in 1963, ostensibly because it did not contribute to its research mission, other postsecondary institutions would firmly establish correspondence study as an alternative teaching and learning method in the meantime. This would subsequently have major implications within higher education for course design and instruction in electronically based formats.

Harper's Headaches: A New Instructional Format in a New University

In his struggle to make correspondence study take root, Harper faced problems familiar to today's practitioners of distance education, whether through correspondence—now typically called "independent study"—or other formats. He faced constant questions about its very legitimacy as a university enterprise. Financing never ceased to be a problem. The faculty found numerous reasons for complaint and resistance. Finally, the aggressive advertising and increasingly flamboyant practices of commercial correspondence schools served to further discredit the instructional method in the eyes of many academics.

Issues of Academic Credibility

Harper had no doubts about the legitimacy of correspondence instruction as a university enterprise. Fully convinced of its efficacy, he promoted it as a means of taking the work of universities beyond campus walls, a goal he believed in absolutely. Yet as he learned in his initial battle with the Chicago faculty, not only were many of his colleagues skeptical about this innovative format, they questioned the wisdom of reaching out to a larger, less scholarly public.

While it is difficult to say why with certainty Professors Laughlin and Hale reacted so vehemently to Harper's plans for correspondence study, simple resistance to challenges to the established order, which reinforced faculty elitism, cannot be ruled out. Moreover, as members of the Cornell faculty, Laughlin and Hale were no doubt familiar with the ill-fated 1883 attempt to found the Correspondence University, a network of professors from institutions around the country who proposed to offer correspondence courses to supplement the work of other institutions. This "university," which failed due to lack of academic credibility, had been headquartered in Ithaca. In addition, Laughlin and Hale had opposed an attempt to establish a statewide extension system in New York (Portman 1978; Storr 1966).

The University of Chicago's Correspondence Study Department acknowledged the general skepticism in its 1900 brochure, noting, "Like all innovations, this one had to establish its right to exist" (p. 1). The brochure asserted that this had been accomplished, citing as proof the number of faculty participants and the thousand students who had enrolled in the previous year. Despite this confident assertion, a general scorn for all extension work, including correspondence study, persisted among Chicago's faculty. In a book entitled *The Higher Learning in America* (1918), the renowned economist Thorstein Veblen savaged Harper, whom he sarcastically called the "Great Pioneer," for "excursions into the public amusement," (p. 16) such as extension. He lamented that:

> a variety of 'university extension' bureaux have been installed, to comfort and edify the unlearned . . . , to dispense erudition by mail order, and to maintain some putative contact with amateur scholars and dilettantes beyond the pale. (pp. 191–192)

Unintended Effects of Policy Decisions

While Harper himself specified in *Official Bulletin, No. 6* that fifty percent of a degree could be earned through correspondence study, he did so in order to promote a balance of formats. It was that seemingly generous allowance that sparked the opposition of Hale and Laughlin. However, as collegiate correspondence study began to expand, the fifty percent policy evolved into a means of limiting correspondence study at Chicago, a way of "holding the line." As other institutions developed correspondence programs, most imposed even lower limits.

Another of Harper's specifications in *Official Bulletin, No. 6* also had the unintended effect of casting doubt upon the legitimacy of the method. He decreed that students could receive academic credit for correspondence courses only by traveling to Chicago to take an examination on campus. Seeking to protect the credibility of the method, Harper thus lessened its effectiveness and utility for students taking their courses at a distance.

Working with the faculty proved not only a constant source of aggravation, but also led to policies that contributed to the erosion of correspondence study's credibility. In his original plans, Harper had proposed an entirely autonomous faculty for Extension. He had expected the professors of the University Proper to make research their first priority and to excel in it. Disseminating knowledge, on the other hand, would be the first priority of the University Extension faculty. He had hoped that this distinction in executing the outreach mission could earn them respect within the University Proper. On the contrary, these plans dissolved and were replaced by other arrangements based on distinctions for Extension professors that led to questions within the university as to their legitimacy as faculty members.

Financial Viability

The funding problems that directly affected all parts of the new university had even greater effects on Extension. For while Harper would go to great expense to round out his faculty in the "University Proper," he insisted that University Extension become financially self-sustaining and frequently pressured its administrators in that regard (Dunkel and Fay 1978). Actually, Correspondence Study, alone of the Extension units, always managed to sustain itself financially. Thus it outlasted the other original departments of University Extension. Even so, Harper always believed that a lack of money kept Correspondence Study from reaching its potential. First, the fees were too high for the program to reach the wide audience he envisioned, and, secondly, the range of courses was too narrow. A liberal endowment would be necessary to correct these flaws, he said in 1903. However, although Harper was an accomplished fund raiser, other projects always took priority (Harper 1903; Dunkel and Fay 1978).

The continuous financial problems quickly ended Harper's dual faculty dream. Instead, a combination of faculty from the University Proper, graduate students, part-time instructors, and a few full-time Extension faculty (identifiable by the tag "Non-Resident," e.g. Non-Resident Assistant in History) staffed Correspondence Study. Over time, this mixture would result in a great deal of tension as to whether certain individuals were, or were not, bona fide members of the faculty (Gerrity 1976).

Faculty Prerogatives

Initially, Harper seemingly had to involve himself in every faculty dispute or problem, no matter how trivial. When unnamed "officers of the university" expressed vague concerns about the quality of an anthropology course, he apparently made a discreet inquiry of the professor, Frederick Starr. Starr reacted angrily. He described the content of the course and vigorously defended its content and rigor. While he resented the criticism from people whom he believed had not examined the course and did not know what they were talking about, Starr said, "I shall withdraw the course at once." After all, he continued, "I hate correspondence study" (University of Chicago, Box 20, Folder 10). Harper was unable to conciliate, and Starr did, in fact, terminate the course (Correspondence Study Department 1901).

Faculty workloads and work habits also took their toll on the correspondence study program. Assistant Professor of Education George Locke asked to be relieved of correspondence duties because of his heavy daytime course load. Harper implored him to use his correspondence earnings to hire a secretary so that he could carry on. Not only had Locke's correspondence courses already been announced, but, "some distinguished gentlemen are enrolling this year . . ." (University of Chicago, Box 20, Folder 10). Harper even involved himself in such insignificant matters as reproaching faculty members who did not return student work promptly. In one case he embarrassed himself while attending to this chore. After having received numerous complaints about the tardiness of a female English instructor, Porter Lander MacClintock, Harper wrote to her husband, an English professor and the dean of University College, asking if something could be done about his wife's work (University of Chicago, Box 20, Folder 10). Mrs. MacClintock replied. While she expressed her deep regard for Harper, she told him firmly:

> You must permit me, my dear President, to say that as a professional person I stand upon my own feet. I am not even "a wife of a member of the faculty" when I am a teacher. I cannot consent to have such an interpretation put upon my relation to the University. It is utterly unjust and humiliating to me and it is most embarrassing to my husband. His very nearness to me makes it impossible for him to represent me. (University of Chicago, Box 20, Folder 10)

She then said she intended to resign her position. In his reply, which he wrote on the same day, Harper apologized for giving offense and invited Mrs. MacClintock to visit him to discuss the matter (University of Chicago, Box 20, Folder 10).

After Harper's death in 1905, relations between the correspondence study administrators and the faculty continued to be a problem; in fact, they worsened as Extension and part-time faculty found themselves increasingly isolated. Their status had never really been on a par with that of the University Proper, despite Harper's best attempts. Without Harper as a champion, they became marginal figures on a research-oriented campus.

The Proprietary School Specter

The University of Chicago did not possess the only large and growing correspondence program of the 1890s. At the same time Harper was establishing correspondence study as a collegiate teaching format, Pennsylvanian Thomas J. Foster had begun to convert a single course in mine safety into a diversified training school with thousands of students. In 1901, Foster incorporated this enterprise, previously known as the Scranton Schools, into the International Correspondence Schools (ICS), then—as now—the largest proprietary correspondence study institution in the world (MacKenzie, Christensen, and Rigby 1968).

Hundreds of other schools quickly followed the Scranton Schools. Most were small and short-lived. Some were fraudulent. All avidly pursued money. Many used extravagant advertising and made impossible promises of success to potential students. Harper, who had never made any money from correspondence study—neither personally nor on behalf of the institutions that sponsored his work—disliked this development.

In spite of his distaste for the proprietary schools, Harper found himself inextricably linked to them. In 1885, writing a famous essay on correspondence study for Bishop Vincent's book on Chautauqua, he had made two enthusiastic statements that would follow him for the rest of his life:

> The student who has prepared a certain number of lessons in the correspondence-school knows more of the subject treated in those lessons, and knows it better, than the student who has covered the same ground in the class-room.

> The day is coming when the work done by correspondence will be greater in amount than that done in the class-rooms of our academies and colleges; when the students who shall recite by correspondence will far outnumber those who make oral recitations. (pp. 192-193)

The proprietary enterprises, most importantly the Scranton Schools, made lavish use of these passages in their advertising in an obvious attempt to gain credibility through association with his name, reputation, and title. A Mr. C. F. Moofe tore an ad for the Scranton Schools out of his local newspaper in Manitowoc, Wisconsin and sent it to Harper. The ad stated:

President Harper of the Chicago University claims that students prepared by correspondence receive more thorough instruction than those prepared by classroom study. (University of Chicago, Box 20, Folder 10)

Mr. Moofe said, apparently sincerely,

I have a son I want to educate and if the correspondence course is better than the class room I can save considerable by giving him the former. Have you been correctly quoted? (University of Chicago, Box 20, Folder 10)

Harper hedged. He said that while correspondence instruction might be as good as that in the classroom, college work went beyond instruction, and "further, the Scranton Schools are conducting this work for money, and not for the purpose of giving instruction (University of Chicago, Box 20, Folder 10). Similar ad copy continued to appear years after Harper's death.

One fledgling proprietary school president actually asked Harper to endorse his venture, Chicago Correspondence Schools, because his name would attract numerous additional endorsements from public school superintendents. This correspondence entrepreneur added that he had used Harper's praise for the correspondence method in his prospectus (University of Chicago, Box 20, Folder 10). Harper declined the request, saying, "I am afraid that you are asking too much of me" (University of Chicago, Box 20, Folder 10). The president of one college would not ask the president of another for an endorsement, he said, and the same should be true of the people in charge of correspondence schools.

The emergence of the proprietary schools as a force in American education did the collegiate programs no good. Their flamboyant and often misleading advertising no doubt reinforced faculty distaste for this most democratic means of teaching. Respected critics of American education, like Veblen, would use the poor reputations of the proprietary schools as a form of guilt-by-association to vindicate faculty snobbery with respect to acceptable forms of instruction, and to disparage the entire method, especially in a collegiate setting.

Harper's Headaches Revisited

Over the century since Harper brought distance education into the modern university, legitimacy has never ceased to be an issue for the advocates and critics of collegiate-level correspondence study, or "independent study" as it is now known. Zealous university registrars continue to monitor limitations on the hours of credit that can be applied to a degree as "safeguards" against a lowering of quality. Such rules endure despite decades of studies that have failed to establish the superiority of conventional classroom instruction.

Enduring Issue #1: Credit Restrictions

In its most recent research profile, the Independent Study Division of the National University Continuing Education Association (NUCEA) reported that 66% of the eighty responding institutions with independent study programs enforce a limitation of 50% or fewer credit hours toward a degree. Forty-three percent of respondents allow a maximum of 25% of credit hours earned through independent study (NUCEA 1994). Further, many colleges and universities apply all correspondence courses—even those they themselves offer—against the transfer course limit. Such absurdities, that defy logic, continue to exist in the name of quality.

As other distance education formats have begun to realize their potential, the question of academic legitimacy has become a much larger topic. Various bodies outside universities have involved themselves in policy making. The Southern Association of Colleges and Schools, for example, now has guidelines for distance education and other regional associations are beginning to demonstrate an interest.

Graduate-level study using distance education methods is infinitely more restrictive than undergraduate course work. Few conventional universities will accept any correspondence course toward a graduate degree, even when offered by their own institutions. The few that do maintain drastic strictures. At The University of Iowa, for example, a graduate student in the College of Education may take up to eight hours by correspondence, but only after admission.

Many university-level distance education programs were designed specifically for the graduate level. Yet, there remains an uneasiness in the graduate college, the agency in every university that proclaims itself the gatekeeper of standards and proudly asserts, "nothing should ever be done for the first time." In 1993, Carla Montgomery, Associate Dean of the Graduate College at Northern Illinois University, warned her colleagues not to be fooled by new wrinkles on the old format:

> Technological advances have expanded the means and media of information exchange. To the extent that some remote-delivery mechanisms are essentially the electronic equivalent of the correspondence-course-by-mail, schools may ban these types of remote-delivery course work for graduate credit, and/or the inclusion of such work in graduate programs. Aside from concerns about academic integrity of correspondence work, there are again fundamental concerns about quality. (1993, 2)

Enduring Issue #2: Funding

Money has never ceased to be a substantial problem for independent study programs, and, now, in other forms of distance education. In the past, a shortage of resources, due mainly to the self-sustaining funding model, had an undeniable impact on quality. Michael Moore noted in 1990 that the problem of restricted funds had resulted in study guides that were too cheap and insubstantial to represent adequate teaching tools. Moore was probably correct.

Recently, however, affordable desktop publishing, better professional staffs in many offices, and the inclusion of other forms of media into correspondence study have gone a long way toward solving this problem. Indeed, correspondence study programs are often in better financial shape than other forms of distance education. In fact, many institutions regularly raid the independent study unit's treasury for the benefit of more expensive electronic media projects.

On the national level, Ambassador Annenberg's 1989 decision to pull his funding from the Corporation for Public Broadcasting has had a profound negative effect on the production and distribution of broadcast telecourses. The State of Iowa's excellent fiber optic network seems perpetually imperiled by financial problems. The legislature's reluctance to adequately fund this project and its constant threats to sell it to private business are holding back its completion and threatening to make it too expensive for educational use.

Enduring Issue #3: Faculty Skepticism

The problems of working with a volunteer faculty, many of whom begrudge the service mission of the university, and others of whom have a marginal status within the academy, seem to have changed hardly at all since Harper's time. Any contemporary director of independent study has probably faced all of the petty faculty problems Harper involved himself in, from late grading to complaining about work loads.

In addition, the faculty beyond those who participate in distance education programs have continued to involve themselves in the issues of legitimacy and quality. In Harper's day—and for the most part since then—many professors have supported restrictions on the use of distance education. While the ideal of quality leads the list of expressed reasons, it is equally likely, but harder to document, that many professors find the demonstrated efficiencies of distance education threatening to their livelihood. Harper's statement about the number of people enrolling in correspondence study eventually exceeding that of resident students almost certainly vexed some academics of the late nineteenth century.

Both issues—academic quality and job security—converged in Maine in 1995. Angry faculty members forced the University's chancellor to resign, due to his aggressive implementation of a separate distance education institution. The head of the faculty union summed up his group's reservations about distance education in a statement that included both lofty concern about standards and self-centered anxiety:

> We'll support it [distance education] if it provides quality of education and doesn't put our positions in jeopardy (Honan 1995).

Enduring Issue #4: Guilt by Association

The specter of the worst of the proprietary schools has remained since Harper's time as a force that taints distance teaching formats. After seventy years of collegiate correspondence study, Charles Wedemeyer and Gayle Childs, the two most honored practitioners of the craft, called the negative image created by some of the commercial schools the greatest single hindrance to the expansion of collegiate independent study. But they conceded that many—if not most—of the proprietaries were reputable concerns (1961).

The folklore about proprietary schools has remained an issue, even though the horror stories about "matchbook universities" are decades out of date. In fact, some of the most innovative and impressive developments in distance education are taking place in the proprietary sector. Yet, there are a few unscrupulous operators who persist in giving the field a bad name, and thus provide the self-appointed guardians of "standards" an excuse to unduly restrict the use of independent study. These guardians of standards do not, of course, require much of an excuse.

Conclusion: Harper's Legacy for Policymakers

The escalating growth of collegiate distance education courses and enrollments in the last two decades has given prominence to a number of enduring inter- and intra-institutional policy issues. Variations of most of these issues have been around since William Rainey Harper first institutionalized distance education, in the form of correspondence study, at the University of Chicago.

Shortages of money, marginal faculty status, never-ending questions about the legitimacy of learning formats that differ from the traditional lecture hall, and that always convenient whipping boy, the proprietary correspondence school, continue to distract educators from fully developing the potential of all forms of distance education. If Harper could visit us today, he would no doubt be gratified by the scale of the diffusion of knowledge through distance education. The tenacity of faculty perceptions of distance education as a threat to their definitions of academic quality and appropriate workloads would, however, come as no surprise to him.

References

Division of Independent Study, NUCEA 1994. Independent Study Program Profiles, 1993-1994.

Dunkel, H. B., and M. A. Fay. 1978. Harper's disappointment: University extension. *Adult Education* 29(1):4–16.

Gerrity, T. W. 1976. College-sponsored correspondence instruction in the United States: A comparative history of its origins (1873-1915) and its recent developments (1960-1975). Ed.D. dissertation. Teachers College, Columbia University, New York.

Harper, W. R. 1903. The president's quarterly statement. *University Record* July:43.

Honan, W. H. 1995. Professors battling television technology. *New York Times.*

Hulbert, E. B. 1906. The Morgan Park period. *The Biblical World* 27:173–174.

MacKenzie, O., E. L. Christensen, and P. H. Rigby. 1968. *Correspondence Instruction in the United States.* New York: McGraw Hill.

Montgomery, C. W. 1993. Some issues in the remote delivery of graduate course work and programs. Paper delivered at the Illinois Association of Graduate Schools. December.

Moore, M. G. 1990. Correspondence study. *Adult Learning Methods.* Malabar, FL: Krieger.

Portman, D. N. 1978. *The Universities and the Public: A History of Higher Education in the United States.* Chicago: Nelson-Hall.

President's Papers, University of Chicago.

Storr, J. S. 1966. Harper's University: *The Beginnings.* Chicago: The University of Chicago Press.

University of Chicago. 1900. *Correspondence Instruction.* Brochure.

University of Chicago. 1901. Correspondence-Study department. *Circular of Information,* 1901-1902 2–3.

University of Chicago. 1891. *Official Bulletin, No. 1.*

University of Chicago. 1892. *Official Bulletin, No. 6.*

Veblen, T. 1918. *The Higher Learning in America: A Memorandum on the Conduct of Universities by Business Men.* New York: N. E. Huebsch.

Vincent, J. H. 1885. *The Chautauqua Movement.* Freeport, NY: Books for Libraries Press.

Warren, R. P. 1946. *All the King's Men.* New York: Grosset & Dunlap.

Wedemeyer, C. A., and G. B. Childs. 1961. *New Perspectives in University Correspondence Study.* Chicago: Center for the Study of Liberal Education for Adults.

4 Faculty Incentives and Rewards for Distance Teaching

Linda L. Wolcott

Introduction

It is timely that we look at teaching incentives and rewards if we are to encourage and support the participation of faculty in distance education programs. How to increase job satisfaction and enhance performance within the institutional culture continues to challenge higher education. With an increase in the use of telecommunication technologies to deliver instruction, together with the demand for greater access to higher education by an increasingly diverse population, the growth of continuing and distance education programs is inevitable. Given the poor track record of rewards in continuing education and their lack of integration with institutional reward systems (Scott 1984), incentives and rewards for distance teaching become an important issue.

The issue of incentives and rewards for distance teaching can be approached through greater understanding of: 1) current reward practices in higher education; 2) the context of faculty performance, satisfaction, and reward; 3) findings from research on incentives and rewards in distance education; and 4) promising directions for future research.

Institutional Rewards and Faculty Motivation

Since the beginning of the decade there has been considerable interest in examining the reward and recognition structures in higher education. Influenced by both external and internal factors, the climate for college teaching has been changing (Edgerton 1993). There are external pressures for colleges and universities to do more with less and to improve undergraduate education, faculty accountability, and productivity. Within higher education, there is greater attention to concerns expressed in three prominent areas: 1) the tendency to undervalue teaching; 2) discrepancies in faculty compensation; and 3) increasing evidence of stress among faculty.

In this changing academic climate, many institutions are re-examining faculty priorities and reward practices in an attempt to better align faculty performance with institutional missions. The practices and policies through which institutions of higher education recognize, reward, and promote academic performance constitute the institutional reward system. In an operational way, this system of incentives and rewards functions to convey institutional values and goals (Lonsdale 1993). Traditionally, the reward system has focused on monetary compensation and the expectation of retention, promotion, and tenure that comprise the basic structural elements upon which the system is built. More recently, scrutiny of institutional reward systems has identified a number of problems with the current practice of rewarding and recognizing faculty for their academic performance:

- Institutions emphasize extrinsic rewards as a way to motivate faculty.
- Institutional reward structures fail to provide for intrinsic rewards.
- Institutional reward systems contain disincentives.
- Faculty perceive reward practices as inequitable.

Motivation. A brief look at the theory behind work motivation illustrates why these practices pose problems. Motivation is a complex process involving three major sets of variables: individual differences in needs, values, perceptions; job attributes; and work environment factors. Numerous theories explain various aspects of employee motivation and work behavior. Although Lonsdale (1993) notes that there is no definitive model that explains the motivation of academic staff, exchange theories of motivation provide a framework for understanding the nature of institutional reward and recognition systems in higher education.

Expectancy/valence theory (Vroom 1964) describes motivation as a relationship between inputs and outcomes. An individual's performance is seen as a function of the extent to which he or she expects that a "certain action [input] will result in a particular outcome" (Steers and Porter 1979, 212). This expectancy measured against the value (valence) that the individual places on that outcome determines the individual's motivational force to perform. Faculty inputs include the effort individuals invest in their education and the activities associated with teaching, research, and service. Outcomes expected as a result of such scholarship include commensurate salary, promotion, and the awarding of tenure among other perquisites.

Equity theory (Adams 1963, 1965) adds another dimension to the relationship between motivation and performance. Equity is expressed as a ratio of an individual's inputs to outcomes as compared to the perceived ratio of similar inputs and outcomes of other individuals or groups. The individual evaluates the relationship by weighing the inputs contributed to and outcomes resulting from the exchange relative to his or her needs and values. The exchange is perceived as equitable when the compared ratios are equal; inequity exists when they are not. Neumann and Finaly-Neumann (1990) describe equity theory at work in an academic setting.

> Faculty members enter work situations and make various investments in as well as contributions to the university. The university [in exchange] is expected by faculty members to provide a supportive environment that facilitates the realization of these investments (skills, abilities, and needs) and a work compensation system that is equitable in rewarding these contributions. To the extent that the university is perceived to provide a supportive environment and an equitable reward system, faculty commitment is likely to increase and vice versa. This exchange perspective suggests that faculty commitment to their university is largely a function of social support at work and equity. (pp. 77-78)

The degree of equity or inequity that an individual perceives in the work environment is related to his/her effort, performance, and job satisfaction. These three elements are important factors in the motivation dynamic, but their interrelationship is complex. Whether satisfaction causes performance or performance causes satisfaction has been widely debated, but the variable that determines their association is the administration of rewards. Effort, then, is a function of several aspects of rewards: the perceived value and equity of the reward, the magnitude of the reward, and the perceptions that greater effort will lead to higher performance and higher performance will lead to rewards.

Intrinsic and Extrinsic Rewards. The locus of the motivation must also be considered in understanding the process of motivation. When behavior is prompted by forces internal to the individual and task accomplishment is controlled by him/her, then the person is said to be intrinsically motivated. Under these conditions, the individual engages in activities to satisfy personal needs regardless of external rewards. When one's behavior is motivated by external factors such as the prospect of merit pay or promotion, then motivation is said to be extrinsic. Individuals are simultaneously motivated by a combination of extrinsic and intrinsic factors that can vary over time (Lonsdale 1993).

Rewards associated with work behavior play a significant role in determining and sustaining motivation. They are instrumental in defining the interactions among effort, performance, and satisfaction. To the extent that institutional reward systems accommodate a range of both extrinsic and intrinsic rewards and are perceived as both equitable and supportive of individual's varying motivations, motivation is enhanced (Neumann and Finaly-Neumann 1990). When they are not, the administration of rewards can lead to dissatisfaction, or worse, act as de-motivating factors or disincentives to performance.

In basing reward systems on external incentives, institutions of higher education have ignored the fact that individuals derive greater satisfaction from intrinsic than from extrinsic rewards. "The development of commitment and enhancement of performance is more likely through a working environment in which intrinsic and socially derived satisfactions are obtained" (Lonsdale 1993, 233). Faculty satisfaction results from six basic incentives as identified by Smart (1978): family, research, administrative advancement, interpersonal, academic recognition, and teaching. Colleges and universities have traditionally neglected to capitalize on the intrinsic nature of motivation (Newell and Spear 1983). While they can contribute to satisfaction, external rewards alone cannot improve or sustain an individual's performance; both intrinsic and extrinsic rewards should be part of the reward structure.

Reliance on extrinsic rewards has negative consequences for faculty motivation. "Not receiving expected external rewards, or working conditions which inhibit the receipt of intrinsic or social satisfactions, can have a de-motivating effect with consequent negative effects on performance" (Lonsdale 1993, 233). For example, Fairweather (1993) documented a negative relationship between teaching and compensation: the more time spent on teaching, the lower the basic salary; those who spend more time on research are rewarded with higher salaries.

The unintended result of a lop-sided reward structure has been that, with respect to teaching, faculty effort and performance are under-rewarded. The scholarly consensus is that systems over-emphasize research and under-value teaching. On most campuses, a climate has developed that pits the intrinsic rewards of teaching against the external rewards of research and publication. Faculty members are rewarded for that which is less likely to lead to improved performance or enhanced job satisfaction. Faculty adapt themselves to doing those things that the institution values (i.e., extrinsical rewards) (Colbeck 1992). Thus, younger faculty are "socialized" to spend little time on teaching (Fairweather 1993). The lack of congruence between personal goals and institutional values can lead to de-motivation (Lonsdale 1993) and contributes to the faculty perception that achieving promotion or tenure depends on research, not teaching.

The problems associated with institutional reward systems led Ernest Boyer, president of the Carnegie Foundation for the Advancement of Teaching, to conclude that "the faculty reward system must give greater recognition to those who teach" (1990, 14). He is not alone in his conviction; other influential observers of academe (cf., Edgerton 1993; Diamond 1993) attest to the urgency of examining faculty reward issues.

> Important faculty work is not being rewarded. Service, teaching, and creativity are risky priorities for faculty members seeking promotion or tenure at many institutions....[T]he focus on research and publication and the mad dash for federal funds and external grants has diverted energies away from important faculty work and has a direct and negative impact on the quality of classroom instruction and the ability of institutions to provide support to and involve their communities. (Diamond 1993, 19)

As the re-examination continues to focus attention on inequities in existing reward systems, institutions have begun to reflect on and redefine scholarly work, to adopt flexible promotion criteria, and to apply different measures of scholarship based on faculty roles and disciplines. Many issues remain, but what is certain is that institutions must provide rewards that are both adequate and equitable to maintain a vigorous professoriate.

Incentives and Rewards in Distance Education

The problems associated with current reward practices in higher education are magnified in distance education. Incentives and rewards have been a long standing issue with respect to motivation and equitable treatment of faculty participating in continuing education or engaging in technology-based classroom innovations. Continuing education, from which distance education emerged, has a history of limited funding and poor rewards that has posed barriers to programming and deterred growth and innovation (Scott 1984). Particularly in the area of monetary compensation, lack of equitable extrinsic rewards has influenced faculty attitudes and motivation to participate. Involvement in continuing education traditionally has not been widely recognized in retention, promotion, and tenure considerations. Indeed, participation in such activities often becomes a disincentive (Scott 1984; Patton 1975). In the current climate of re-examination of academic reward structures, motivating faculty through equitable rewards is a major challenge in continuing education (Smith 1991).

Rewards with respect to innovation, particularly technological innovation, are likewise a timely and important issue. Though extrinsic factors are linked to the adoption of technological innovations (Callas 1982; Kozma 1979), rewards for such innovation have been incompatible with traditional academic values (McNeil 1990). *The Chronicle of Higher Education* reports that technology-related issues are a high priority with higher education members of both the National Education Association and the American Federation of Teachers (Blumenstyk 1993). Indeed, some institutions reward technology-based work such as developing software and publishing in electronic journals (DeLoughry 1993). Innovation should be rewarded, yet the continued uncertainty of rewards makes involvement in classroom innovations such as distance education a risky proposition for faculty.

Reward Practices and Policies. Apart from attitudes and perceptions, little is known about current reward practices and policies for distance teaching in higher education. Wolcott and Haderlie (in progress) are studying the practices of eighty-five western colleges and universities. Their goal is to identify the types of incentives and rewards, and to describe their relationship to institutional reward structures.

What do we know about incentives and rewards in distance education? Faculty development issues in this arena have not been widely addressed. In their review of research relating to faculty issues in distance education, Dillon and Walsh (1992) characterize the literature as "lacking in quality and quantity" (p. 15). With respect to rewards and incentives, they conclude that the problems in distance education are similar to those of institutional reward systems in general:

1. *"Faculty perceive distance teaching as less rewarding, offering fewer career advantages, and less scholarly than other teaching activities"* (p. 10). Differences in perception separate administrators who believe that their departments or institutions adequately and equitably reward distance teaching and faculty who do not.

2. *Institutional commitment to distance education is lacking.* Identified policies and practices in support of distance teaching vary widely across institutions. "In fact, the research portrays institutions as largely indifferent, inconsistent, and skeptical, and as operating in an environment in which distance education is considered, at best, peripheral to the 'real' mission of the institution" (p. 16).

3. *Conflicting perceptions and lack of institutional commitment notwithstanding, faculty do not participate in distance teaching for extrinsic rewards.* Rather, they are motivated more by intrinsic rewards such as self-esteem; opportunities for professional development, innovation, or research; greater visibility; enriching their teaching; and being of greater assistance to students and the university community.

Six studies undertaken since Dillon and Walsh's 1992 review reinforce and elaborate on several of their conclusions. Clark (1993) built on the work of Dillon (1989) by investigating the attitudes and perceptions of higher education faculty toward distance education. His findings give added credence to the perception that distance teaching is not well rewarded. Fewer than half of the respondents indicated that they believed their institution would adequately reward participation in distance education activities. While faculty believed that distance teaching should be rewarded in the same way as other teaching activities, those who perceived distance teaching as insufficiently rewarded based their doubts on perceptions of inadequate financial rewards; workload, research, and publication concerns; and distrust of administrators.

Recent research amplifies on these barriers to participation in distance education and sheds additional light on the interaction between the institutional environment for distance education and faculty attitudes. Walsh (1993) concluded that the faculty's attitude toward distance education is composed of interrelated factors that include: (a) barriers to and incentives for engaging in distance education, and (b) opportunities and support for distance teaching. Similarly, Clark (1993) reported that faculty mentioned such barriers to participation as "administrative, technical, economic, and student support obstacles to distance teaching" (p. 30). The absence of faculty incentives was a barrier to the adoption of digital compressed video technology at one institution (Bolduc 1993).

Shattuck and Zirger (1993) explored faculty incentive policies at universities that offered outreach engineering education programs. They focused on the amount and method of compensation provided to faculty for teaching either college credit or non-credit continuing education courses. It was concluded that "the driving forces for faculty participation in distance education programs are traditions [the historical role of and emphasis placed on distance education in the institution] and incentives" (p. 4).

Among Shattuck and Zirger's (1993) recommendations are strategies for creating a tradition of distance education that strengthens institutional commitment and decreases the marginality of distance teaching. They recommend the following institutional actions: 1) write a statement of commitment to and support for distance education; 2) establish a policy that places appropriate weight on distance education assignments in promotion, tenure, and salary decisions; 3) establish a protocol to facilitate faculty involvement in distance education programs; 4) adjust teaching assignments to compensate for increases in workload; and 5) expand existing financial incentives and develop new ones such as funding for the preparation of instructional materials, support for teaching assistants, and direct payments to faculty who participate in distance education.

There is additional evidence that faculty participate in distance education primarily for intrinsic reasons (Bolduc 1993; Clark 1993; Jackson 1994). Jackson identified five incentives that currently encourage agricultural science faculty to plan and deliver distance education courses. These faculty were motivated by such intrinsic and service incentives as: 1) having additional use of the instructional materials beyond the distance education course; 2) more efficiently delivering instruction; 3) more efficiently reaching larger audiences; 4) increasing public interest in a topic; and 5) more efficiently responding to public requests for information.

The respondents to Jackson's (1994) Delphi study identified further incentives that, if offered, would enhance faculty participation in distance education. Reflective of the actions recommended by Shattuck and Zirger (1993), these incentives included four extrinsic rewards: 1) recognition from administrators, peers, and clientele; 2) funding to produce courses; 3) adequate support staff for course production; and 4) time to plan and deliver a course or program.

Research relating to faculty incentives and rewards for distance teaching is in its nascent stage. Yet, the number of recent studies reflects the ground swell of interest in issues related to rewarding faculty performance. Studies with respect to incentives and rewards for distance teaching are improving in quality. Variations in methodology include case study and other qualitative procedures. Larger sample sizes representative of diverse institutions and programs give greater validity and generalizability to findings. Despite these advances, several limitations that persist in the literature of the past two years include: 1) researchers' primarily United States perspective, and 2) neglect by researchers of institutional efforts such as faculty development and instructional services. At this writing, however, Wolcott and Haderlie are examining a range of rewards that include institutional support for distance teaching.

The major conclusions derived from the literature review still hold true. Recent studies continue to document a disparity between the tenets of motivation theory and contemporary faculty reward practices in higher education. Research to date offers little comfort that distance teaching is gaining in status within the academy. Studies continue to depict distance education as an endeavor outside the mainstream of institutional reward systems. Distance teaching faculty remain disenfranchised as second class citizens caught up in a system that fails to fairly compensate and sufficiently reward academic performance, especially teaching. As Parer and colleagues (1988) point out, this problem stems in part from the fact that "distance education has been grafted onto the conventional educational system" (p. 1).

Directions for Future Research

The resurgence of interest in work motivation in higher education raises important issues about promoting and acknowledging scholarly work. In relation to distance education, in particular, questions arise about job satisfaction; congruence among institutional mission, goals, and reward practices; motivational factors and barriers to faculty participation; and equitable compensation, support, and recognition. We are only beginning to explore the territory that will lead to greater understanding of the incentives and rewards for distance teaching. There is a need for on-going empirical investigations that focus on policies and practices, and on the locus of motivation for distance teaching. To this end, research is needed in the following areas.

Motivational Factors. Lonsdale (1993) predicted that extrinsic rewards will continue to predominate as higher education applies such business practices as merit pay. Consequently, a better understanding is needed of the role of extrinsic rewards in motivating faculty to participate in distance education.

Available research leaves open the role of extrinsic rewards. How effective are these rewards? Are some extrinsic factors more highly associated with motivation and performance than others? What is the relationship between intrinsic and extrinsic rewards from a faculty viewpoint? Is there a "right" or optimal combination of rewards? With what intrinsic factors might institutions attract faculty to and sustain them in distance teaching? Equally important, what factors act as disincentives to further participation in distance teaching?

Monetary Compensation and Financial Incentives. Research documents considerable variation and discrepancy in compensating higher education faculty. Those whose roles emphasize teaching typically receive lower pay than those primarily engaged in research (Fairweather 1993). Likewise, faculty are poorly rewarded for service, a designation often applied to continuing and distance education activities. What patterns can be identified in compensating distance teaching faculty? Are there significant differences across academic disciplines and ranks? Do faculty teaching through a particular delivery mode fare better than their colleagues? Are inequities for junior faculty members, minorities, and part-time faculty compounded in distance teaching? To what extent are stipends based on enrollment, number of sites, or academic discipline? Besides salary, how common are financial incentives such as travel grants, cash awards for excellence in distance teaching, or funding for course development?

Institutional Support Practices and Activities. Faculty development and instructional support services vary widely across campuses, yet such services are important for faculty vitality and productivity. Faculty participating in innovative instructional practices such as distance teaching often need technical support and instructional assistance. How widespread and integral to instruction are support services that target distance teachers? What models are most successful? Are production assistance and training part of the infrastructure that supports distance education? Do practices serve the needs of both senior and less experienced faculty? What forms of institutional support and faculty development are effective? Are faculty typically assigned teaching assistants to handle large enrollments of widely dispersed students? What role do site facilitators play? Do site facilitators serve effectively as the distance teacher's eyes and ears?

Reward Structures and Institutional Priorities. Research on incentives and rewards places distance education on the periphery of higher education, where it is perceived as neither integral to the institutional mission nor equitably reflected in reward and recognition practices. Are these perceptions valid? Additional research is needed which focuses less on attitudes and more on behaviors to accurately describe the relationship between distance education and institutional reward structures. Do reward practices accommodate distance teaching activities? How, in fact, are distance teachers rewarded or not rewarded? Is a faculty member's involvement in distance education an asset or a liability? Such questions are critical in determining the effect of current practices on faculty recruitment, retention, and advancement.

Information Technologies. The newest issues facing the academy at large relate to the use of information technologies to deliver instruction and disseminate scholarly work. Institutions will have to address faculty concerns about extra compensation, royalties, and the rights of ownership of intellectual property for courses developed for electronic delivery (Blumenstyk 1993). Redefining scholarship and the appropriate ways to promote and reward it calls for institutions to consider the legitimacy of work published in other than traditionally accepted outlets and formats. These issues will figure prominently in the on-going inquiry into incentives and rewards in distance education.

Conclusion

At present, distance education suffers from a lack of integration with institutional reward systems. The absence of appropriate incentives for distance teaching continues to hold back participation (Dillon 1989; Jackson 1994). In addition, there is "no culture of established norms, skills and rewards for distance education" (Parer, Croker, and Shaw 1988, 1). Until we define and develop an appropriate distance teaching reward system on its own terms, those engaged in teaching at a distance must function within the ambiguities of the existing structure.

As the movement to examine faculty reward practices in higher education gains momentum, there could be no better climate in which to focus on rewards for distance teaching. It is time for researchers to influence the larger debate within the academy by placing concerns about distance education incentives and rewards on the agenda. By contributing to more informed practice, we can help distance education realize its potential to provide greater and more open access to quality education for all citizens.

References

Adams, J. S. 1963. Toward an understanding of inequity. *Journal of Abnormal and Social Psychology* 67:422–436.

Adams, J. S. 1965. Inequity in social exchange. In *Advances in Experimental Social Psychology,* vol. 2, ed. L. Berkowitz, 267–299. New York: Academic Press.

Blumenstyk, G. 1993. Networks to the rescue? *Chronicle of Higher Education* 14 December:A21–25.

Bolduc, W. J. 1993. The diffusion of digital compressed video-interactive in an university environment, 1988-92: A case study. Dissertation Abstracts International 54 A4294.

Boyer, E. 1990. *Scholarship Reconsidered: Priorities of the Professoriate.* Princeton, NJ: Carnegie Foundation for the Advancement of Teaching.

Callas, D. 1982. Rewards and classroom innovations. *Community College Review* 10(2):13–18.

Clark, T. 1993. Attitudes of higher education faculty toward distance education: A national survey. *The American Journal of Distance Education* 7(2):19–33.

Colbeck, C. 1992. Extrinsic rewards and intrinsic interests: The influence of tenure on faculty preferences for teaching or research. Paper presented at the meeting of the Association for the Study of Higher Education, October, Minneapolis, MN. ERIC Document Reproduction Service, ED 352 904.

DeLoughry, T. J. 1993. Professors report progress in gaining recognition for their use of technology. *Chronicle of Higher Education* 3 March:19–21.

Diamond, R. D. 1993. How to change the faculty reward system. *Trusteeship* 1(5):17–21.

Dillon, C. 1989. Faculty rewards and instructional telecommunications: A view from the telecourse faculty. *The American Journal of Distance Education* 3(2):35–43.

Dillon, C. L., and S. M. Walsh. 1992. Faculty: The neglected resource in distance education. *The American Journal of Distance Education* 6(3):5–21.

Edgerton, R. 1993. Re-examination of faculty priorities. *Change* 24(4):10–25.

Fairweather, J. S. 1993. Academic values and faculty rewards. *Review of Higher Education* 17(1):43–68.

Jackson, G. B. 1994. Incentives for planning and delivering agricultural distance education. *Agricultural Education Magazine* February:15–16.

Kozma, R. B. 1979. Communication, rewards, and the use of classroom innovations. *Journal of Higher Education* 50:761–771.

Lonsdale, A. 1993. Changes in incentives, rewards and sanctions. *Higher Education Management* 5(2):223–235.

McNeil, D. R. 1990. *Wiring the Ivory Tower: A Round Table on Technology in Higher Education.* Washington, DC: Academy for Educational Development.

Neumann, Y., and E. Finaly-Neumann. 1990. The reward-support framework and faculty commitment to their university. *Research in Higher Education* 31(1):75–89.

Newell, L. J., and K. I. Spear. 1983. New dimensions for academic careers: Rediscovering intrinsic satisfactions. *Liberal Education* 69:109–16.

Parer, M. S., S. Croker, and B. Shaw. 1988. Institutional support and rewards for academic staff involved in distance education. Victoria, Australia: Centre for Distance Learning, Gippland Institute. ERIC Document Reproduction Service, ED 310 757.

Patton, C. V. 1975. Extended education in an elite institution: Are there enough incentives to encourage faculty participation? *Journal of Higher Education* 66:427–444.

Scott, J. 1984. Faculty compensation in continuing education: Theory versus practice. *Continuum* 48(2):77–89.

Shattuck, K. L., and A. J. Zirger. 1993. Faculty incentives for outreach engineering education programs. Unpublished manuscript, University of Florida.

Smart, J. C. 1978. Diversity of academic organizations: Faculty incentives. *Journal of Higher Education* 49:403–419.

Smith, W. 1991. Leadership challenges in continuing education and extension. *Adult Learning* 3(3):14–16.

Steers, R. M., and L. W. Porter. 1979. *Motivation and Work Behavior* 2nd ed. New York: McGraw-Hill.

Vroom, V. H. 1964. *Work and Motivation.* New York: John Wiley & Sons.

Walsh, S. M. 1993. Attitudes and perceptions of university faculty toward technology-based distance education. Dissertation Abstracts International 54 A781.

5   Effective Partnerships: Key to the Future of Distance Education

Shirley S. Hendrick

Introduction

Effective partnerships will be a key to improving practices in distance education. Three forces help to account for the increasingly important role of partnerships in successful distance education programs: 1) shrinking resources; 2) wider use of sophisticated technology; and 3) faculty time and instructional resources.

Shrinking Resources. There is ample evidence that resources available to higher education are dwindling. Appropriations for postsecondary education institutions have been reduced as public priorities have shifted. There is pressure on faculty to fund a greater portion of their salaries through grants. Faculty are expected to lower their requests for funded professional travel and to document greater productivity as instructors and scholars. These are among the more prominent indicators that higher education institutions must adjust to changed circumstances if they are to live within their means.

Wider Use of Sophisticated Technology. With the increased capabilities of computers, more affordable compressed video technology, and increased access to the Internet, higher education institutions and corporations are designing courses using a multi-media approach. Although these options are generally more affordable than satellite technology, the investment in their use is substantial. Compressed video technology costs approximately \$30,000 to \$50,000 per course unit, a considerably greater investment than chalk and chalkboard, the overhead projector, or the VCRs which have become standard technologies intraditional classrooms.

Until recently, by using print-based course materials or affordable teleconferencing, distance education has been relatively inexpensive compared to the costs of developing and delivering the multi-media courses that are becoming more prevalent. With the greater investment in technology-based courses, there is greater incentive to form partnerships either to spread the cost of the investment over more courses or to share the technology on an "as needed" basis.

Faculty Time and Instructional Resources. A number of authors have recognized the need to develop multi-media courses. Holmberg and Bakshi (1992), in "Postmortem on a Distance Education Course: Successes and Failures," specify the following members of the telecommunications-assisted course development team: author, instructional designer, visual designer, editor, and sometimes course manager, content consultant, a second designer or editor, various illustrators, design and production assistants, secretaries, typesetters, narrators, audio technicians, librarians, and printers. According to Holmberg and Bakshi, it is not uncommon for up to fifteen people to work on one unit of a course. Their assessment is that the specialized expertise contributed by each team member is crucial to producing excellent course materials, and that the positive synergistic effects of several people working on a project produces superior results. Similarly, David Ross (1991), emphasizes the need for a project manager to keep the project moving forward and to control for the performance of teams, time, and costs.

To maximize the benefits of teamwork, higher education institutions will need to develop partnerships to collaborate on the development of quality multi-media courses so that the costs can be spread among a number of institutions. One faculty member who has developed a course to be delivered on video tape estimates that it takes about ten hours to develop a half hour tape. Thus, the costs of developing the multi-media type courses that can be offered at a distance make it nearly imperative to form partnerships.

Corporations plan to select "master teachers" for courses they want to deliver electronically. Similarly, partnerships can provide the resources for faculty to develop multi-media courses for which they have earned the reputation of "master teacher." By forming partnerships, the partners could offer an outstanding program of courses taught by "master teachers" from each partner institution. This, in turn, could lead to increased scrutiny of academic content and methodology and to potential academic competition resulting in a re-examination of policy and administrative practices concerning the development and delivery of telecommunications-based courses.

Ten Behaviors of Successful Partnerships

As we look to increased academic partnerships, it is beneficial to consider some of the research focused on partnerships to better understand the future of distance education. Joanne Sujansky (1991) defines partnering as "two or more individuals working in collaboration toward a desired outcome." She identifies three keys to effective partnering: vision, commitment, and plan of action.

Each partner must have a VISION of their future, and the vision of the partners must be compatible. If one partner's vision is to offer high quality programs, and the other's vision is to design and deliver programs as inexpensively as possible, the partnership is destined for failure.

The second key, COMMITMENT, requires each partner to make every effort to reach their mutually set goals. This can sometimes be difficult given the multiple priorities that each partner may have. Priorities may shift over time, thus making it difficult to continue the efforts toward meeting mutually set goals. This makes it necessary to evaluate the partnership continuously.

The third key, PLAN OF ACTION, is sometimes overlooked in the enthusiasm of working together on a project for which there are, at least initially, high expectations. From a management perspective, partners can either invest time in planning up front or spend time later cleaning up the problems. Careful planning usually increases the probability of a good working relationship.

Sujansky (1991) defines ten behaviors in successful partnerships: *The first behavior is that results are identified.* One avenue to success in partnerships with corporations is to design a certificate program that allows for the university, the corporation, and the students to set short range goals, have a small success, and then determine whether the partnership is beneficial to all partners.

The second behavior is the agreement of the partners to make a difference. If a partnership is developed to provide higher quality programs and the new programs are indistinguishable from those prior to the partnership, the partnership is not making a difference.

Clarifying roles is the third behavior. Even within a single institution, the partnerships formed to design and deliver distance education programs can result in roles that overlap or conflict. Being sure to clarify roles is especially important with international partners where cultural and institutional differences can result in unintended interpretations of agreements.

Assessing needs is the fourth behavior. Considerable exploration is required to determine whether there is a need for a partnership and, if so, what the partners' needs are and how the identified needs will be met by the partnership.

The possibility that needs may support only a short-term partnership should be acknowledged by the partners.

The fifth behavior is recognizing achievements. Students who complete a certificate program are awarded a certificate recognizing their achievement. This not only acknowledges individual accomplishment, but reinforces to the partners, possibly a university and a corporation, that the partnership has "made a difference," achieved a desired "identified result," and validated the roles of each of the partners. Recognizing achievements is particularly important when the partners are at a geographic distance with few occasions for informal communication.

Making ongoing corrections is an important sixth behavior. Adjustments to changed circumstances or to improve outcomes are essential to success. One such partnership, in which the U.S. Peace Corps will offer courses to a group of Russians, will inevitably require ongoing corrections or adjustments.

Willingness to take risks is the seventh behavior. It is much easier to say we do not have the "master faculty" to offer courses for a program, or that we do not have the necessary technology, than to take the risk of developing a partnership that may provide needed resources and yet may not be successful.

The eighth behavior is encourage creativity. This behavior adds to the risk encountered in partnerships. When certificate programs in independent learning are enhanced by technology such as two-way audiovisual sessions, risk is generated. Using the Internet for course work can lead to greater student interaction with the instructor and with each other. Any creative approach carries instruction into uncharted areas where the probability of failure is greater.

Yet, partnerships can mitigate risks as well as increasing them. Sujansky (1991) found that "effective partners develop a relationship that allows for mistakes and encourages learning from them. Partners learn from one another's errors so they can move ahead more effectively. The partners deal with what went wrong so that they can avoid similar mistakes in the future" (p. 16).

Challenging one another is the ninth behavior in successful partnerships. Partners make one another's contributions count and give credit where it is due. By challenging each other, both partners can be more productive and undertake more interesting activities.

The tenth behavior is to evaluate the results and the partnership. It is important to evaluate whether the partnership is accomplishing the partners' goals and objectives. For short-term goals, such as development of a certificate program, each partner can relatively quickly evaluate whether the partnership is meeting their goals. They can then adapt the partnership, end the partnership with a sense of completion, or develop new, more appropriate goals.

Dealbusters

Not all partnerships succeed. Rosabeth Moss Kanter, a scholar with an outstanding career in the study of organizational development, has identified the following critical issues associated with "dealbusters" for partnerships.

Strategic shifts. Kanter (1989), suggests that "strategic shifts" are a critical issue for partnerships. As a university shifts its strategies to use new technologies to deliver distance education programs, partnerships need to be re-evaluated to determine whether they are still viable. New partnerships with like-minded institutions may be needed to develop media-supported programs that can draw on master teachers for all courses.

Uneven level of commitment. If resources are available in one institution to develop a program within two years and a partner institution can provide resources only at a rate that will complete the project in six years, the partnership will be under great strain.

Power imbalance. Power may be in the form of resources or information. When one partner has considerably more control than the other and uses that imbalance to their own benefit, the partnership is in jeopardy. Similarly, an imbalance in information may lead to suspicions that one partner is taking inappropriate advantage of the partnership.

Imbalance of benefits. When one institution has few students who can take advantage of a partnership program compared to another institution, a partnership that required equal contributions of resources may be perceived by the disadvantaged partner as having an imbalance of benefits.

Premature trust. In the enthusiasm of identifying the potential benefits of a partnership, the ability or the commitment of both partners to follow through on the goals or plans may be glossed over. At the outset of a partnership, neither party wants to explore the extent to which each can be trusted since it may be interpreted as a lack of enthusiasm.

Conflicting loyalties. Multiple partnerships can lead to conflicts such as scheduling when resources are insufficient to offer a program to two organizations with identical needs. Even within a single institution internal conflicts can arise over the use of resources for residential programs and distance education courses.

Undermanagement. A lack of understanding of the need to manage a partnership, or the absence of experience in how to manage these arrangements, can be detrimental to the success of a partnership. After the initial enthusiasm of the partnership, day-to-day management can seem quite mundane. Following through on getting textbooks distributed, handling registrations, working with faculty to ensure that audio-visual materials are prepared, collecting fees, and keeping everyone appraised of ongoing activities are sometimes unrecognized as part of the foundation on which the relationship is built.

Hedging on resource allocation. Kanter (1989) also identifies resource allocation as a potential dealbuster. Partners may learn that instead of two individuals to work on a project, only one person will be free to provide assistance. When resources become unavailable or irregular, the partnership will be difficult to sustain.

Insufficient integration. When an institution makes distance education the responsibility of a nonacademic unit, the activity is often perceived within the academy as peripheral to the organization's central mission. As a result, partnerships for distance education may never have the support of the whole institution. Faculty may question the quality of courses delivered electronically. Students may have to take extra steps to have the courses accepted by the institution. Policies or procedures that are inappropriate to telecommunications-based instruction may create additional problems for the partnership.

Lack of a common framework. Do the partners have a shared understanding of the framework for the partnership? Adequate communication and planning are essential to a common understanding of the partnership's mission and goals. This is particularly important in international distance education where there are likely to be social and cultural differences in perspective.

Internal politics. Internal politics must be considered in dealing with issues such as which partner will be credited with the student hours, how the revenue will be distributed, who determines the schedule of courses, how to handle a poor instructor, or the division of responsibility for resources. In addition, a dealbuster not identified by Kanter that is relevant to higher education distance education partnerships is the absence of compatible technology and the lack of expertise in the use of technology. Considering these and the other "dealbusters," one might question the viability of entering into academic partnerships. Yet, partnerships do survive through careful planning and a discriminating choice of partners that takes the dealbusters described by Kanter (1989) into account.

Conclusion

It is important to examine whether the behaviors defined by Sujansky (1991) and the dealbusters described by Kanter (1989) influence higher education partnerships in distance education in the same ways that they have been shown to affect corporate ventures. Are there other behaviors that have not been identified by Sujansky, or additional dealbusters, that are critical to the success of distance education partnerships among postsecondary education institutions? Can investigation of a possible life cycle for partnerships contribute to partners' understanding of the natural evolution of these arrangements if, indeed, there are stages to be anticipated by the partners? Considering the importance of effective partnerships to the future of telecommunications-assisted distance education in higher education, further exploration of factors that influence the success of these collaborations is imperative.

References

Holmberg, R. G., and T. S. Bakshi. 1992. Postmortem on a distance education course: Successes and failures. *The American Journal of Distance Education* 6(1):27–39.

Kanter, R. M. 1989. *When Giants Learn to Dance.* New York: Simon and Schuster.

Ross, D. 1991. Project management in the development of instructional material for distance education: An Australian overview. *The American Journal of Distance Education* 5(2):24–30.

Sujansky, J. 1991. *The Power of Partnering.* San Diego: Pfeiffer & Company.

6 Technology: The Turning Point for Distance Education

Victor Guerra and
Carmen Alvarez-Buylla

Introduction

Recent developments in technology have drastically changed the nature of distance education. Computer networks—especially the Internet—digital videoconferencing, and other multimedia formats permit teachers to use their accustomed approaches, materials, and expertise to realize the same outcomes they have come to expect from traditional classroom methods while teaching students at distant sites. With modern technologies, personal contact is not lost and traditional materials require few modifications. Formats such as digitally compressed videoconferencing make the distance teaching process fully interactive, allowing personal video and audio contact between all participants. The development of new technologies and the consequent decline in costs are providing valuable tools for teachers and learners, significantly expanding the ways in which knowledge can be transmitted. In addition, these technologies can put students in contact with people and information worldwide, thereby obtaining results not available through traditional methods.

At the National University of Mexico (UNAM), our approach features a nationwide distance education program with more than one hundred networked classrooms. Students at local and remote sites attend classes at times compatible with their normal daily activities. We have chosen videoconferencing and computer networks as our primary delivery technologies. Because students experience full interaction, both among themselves and with the teacher, we believe the number of students per class should not exceed that of a traditional classroom.

Fundamental Installations

In or near each videoconferencing classroom are several networked computers that provide traditional services, in addition to those required by the virtual university. This computer center is at the same time post office, library, bookstore, and registrar's office. It is also the traditional computer center that can be used both during a class and as a complement.

Because there are no transportation costs, in either time or money, the best scholars can meet their full potential by teaching students in programs suited to their own (the scholars') interests and qualifications. Professors can lecture from their own laboratories, using their own equipment and collaborating with colleagues and aides.

Promoting the creation of regional academic institutions is a priority in Mexico, where only a few large cities are well developed. The national emphasis on modernization makes the inception and consolidation of highly qualified groups of citizens in smaller cities imperative. The old way—moving students to other cities for their formal education—has had the unintended effect of centralizing the educated population in major urban areas. Distance education methodologies, however, can counteract this trend. Students may remain in their native environments and participate in educational programs through which they can earn undergraduate and graduate degrees. Working professionals can remain in their workplaces and be retrained to incorporate recent developments into their specialties or into other areas needed locally. Without leaving home, they can obtain first-hand knowledge of recent innovations and cutting-edge technology.

In summary, the main reasons for choosing computer networks and videoconferencing as the primary media for distance education are:

- This combination of technologies preserves the high quality of present educational systems, in which teacher and learners have unimpeded interaction in time and space;

- Professors and students study in the same geographic locations where they perform their normal activities;

- Highly specialized scholars, professors, and researchers—all experts in their respective fields—can be used to their full potential;

- The regional technology center creates a virtual space in which students and teachers have access to all services of the modern educational institution; and,

- Instantaneous access to information, people, and worldwide events empowers students, permitting them to benefit from the advantages of the Information Age.

Policy Considerations

From its beginning, distance education in Mexico has focused on providing education for those previously without access to its benefits, for reasons related to cost, occupation, geographical distribution, and even age. In Mexico, excessive population centralization has become a critical problem, in no small part because students attending school or training courses in large cities tend to remain there permanently. In addition, students confront transportation costs and living expenses when they are forced to relocate in order to attend educational institutions. These problems have not changed, but technology offers an increasingly simple means of teaching at distant sites, with direct communication between teachers and learners. Although production procedures remain a major concern, distance education promises improvement in the quantity and quality of the teaching/learning process for people who have previously lacked access to higher education.

It may appear contradictory that we recommend the use of expensive and sophisticated technologies when each classroom serves only around forty students. However, we must remember that quality is not being sacrificed, and the use of this media will add only $30.00 to $50.00 per student, per course. Compared to the economic, social, and political consequences of removing students from their native or professional environments, this is a bargain.

New Ways of Learning

We have argued that videoconferencing is feasible and cost-effective. However, it is also pertinent to expand on the ways in which technology creates new and better ways of learning. Today, most educators criticize methodologies based on rote memorization. Instead, they promote approaches that permit students to construct their own knowledge by confronting alternate theories, interacting with contemporaries, solving actual problems, and carrying out group research and discussions. When teachers try to put these alternate pedagogies into practice within the four-walled classroom, they face limits. One of the most exciting aspects of UNAM's telecommunications media is that these walls disappear and the learning environment opens up. These technologies can unite students, communities, and even nations; they connect students with international libraries, data bases, and virtual museums. Opportunities for accessing information, discussing critical issues, and participating in significant events seem unlimited.

Bi-directional computer networks—in particular the Internet—and videoconferencing make it possible to create a positive attitude and an ideal environment for learning. Factors that initially may not seem important, for example speech accompanied by body language and expression, communicate much more to students and teachers than speech-based instruction alone. This combination creates the optimum atmosphere to transform the student from a passive receptor of information into a collaborator within the academic field.

A project currently underway in UNAM's high school program provides an excellent example of the use of distance education to enhance learning experiences. Students conducting research on the environment recently loaded summaries of their work into an international database on the environment to participate in an international environmental conference held at the Museum of Natural History in New York City, Youth CaN '95. Telecommunications technology from UNAM's Academic Computing Center made this project possible. Through such projects, students can see the impact of their research on the real world. Technology gives them the opportunity to share their work with others worldwide, thus fostering hopes of international cooperation. As an additional benefit, students can reinforce their acquisition of foreign language skills as they interact with the scientific community.

In order to improve the quality and quantity of learning through technology, teachers need to reexamine their roles within the classroom. They are becoming facilitators who help students learn to reflect on both content and the process through which they acquire new knowledge. It is this conscious effort to internalize knowledge that leads to significant learning experiences. The process is guided by the teacher's skill at translating the curriculum into significant tasks, activities, and subtasks for successful learning.

Cooperative learning strategies in which students pool their resources and abilities and assume responsibility for their own and others' learning outcomes are the most productive. In a country facing as many challenges as Mexico, it is important that young people understand the interrelationships between their own futures and those of their community and country, so that they can work together harmoniously to solve problems. In addition to increasing the scope and quality of the learning experience, cooperative learning fosters social skills and teaches students how to work together. These cooperative skills and attitudes are best learned at school; it is improbable that they will be acquired spontaneously in later life.

Because teachers and students work side by side to implement this approach, it is natural for students who excel at technology to help fellow students—or even the teacher—with sophisticated procedures such as file transfers or video hookups. This is one of the reasons why the student work force at the National

University of Mexico plays such an important role in the field of technology. In addition to assisting their teachers, they frequently aid administrators and other faculty to operate the technology. Students thus gain opportunities to develop self-esteem while mastering the technical skills on which the future success of our country depends.

Another relevant use of technology is in the academic field of economics. Students have instantaneous access to international financial databases via the Internet. Rather than working on hypothetical cases, they can use real data to prove or refute their hypotheses. This gives students hands-on practice, no matter where they or their teachers are located. The possibility for this kind of immediate interaction between teachers, students, and databases is one of the most salient aspects of UNAM's new distance education delivery systems.

UNAM-USA Distance Learning and Services On-Line Program

UNAM is proud to announce the opening of a distance learning program in San Antonio jointly sponsored by UNAM's Communications Technology and Academic Computing Systems and its San Antonio-based Permanent Extension School. The program consists of courses, seminars, and lectures—via videoconferencing—from the UNAM campus in Mexico City. The totally interactive videoconferencing medium enables UNAM to offer a diverse range of subjects that would otherwise not be available to students in San Antonio.

The first academic short course, offered in English in May, 1995, consisted of two panel discussions presented by three prominent UNAM scholars who engaged in interactive dialogue with students throughout the course. Entitled "Causes of the Mexican Economic Crisis," the first part looked at the recent 1995 upheaval in the Mexican economy and financial markets and examined the reasons behind events. The second session, "Alternatives and Perspectives for the Mexican Economic Crisis," explored the options facing Mexico and considered future perspectives.

Because of the need to create academic groups of educated citizens in Mexico's smaller cities, UNAM has established a network of 100 classrooms with videoconferencing and Internet facilities. This program usually operates in collaboration with regional universities, and is used for formal and nonformal teaching programs. It includes extensive use of the USA videoconference channel to sponsor collaborative programs with North American academic institutions.

In addition, telecommunicated classrooms (TC) are being installed in schools on UNAM's main campus, as well as on other campuses in Mexico City. Each TC is integrated by a main classroom with the usual videoconferencing equipment—a TV monitor, two or three cameras and one document camera.

One camera covers the teacher and another the students. The computer room contains some five to ten networked computers, several laser printers, and a video projector. The channel that links all the classrooms is an E1 2.048 mbps (divided between 384 kbps for compressed video, with the remainder for Internet); in some places part of the Internet bandwidth is used by one or two telephone lines. One or two technicians aid each Telecampus to provide support for administration and promotional activities. One or more telecommunicated classrooms will also be installed in almost all state capitals.

Conclusion

The University has dedicated a large portion of its budget to the development of a national telecommunications infrastructure and to the training of teachers and researchers in its use. Videoconferencing and computer networks in distance learning programs will bring education to those currently deprived of postsecondary education and help to slow the massive migrations of young, trained, and talented citizens towards the country's largest cities. In this way, the National University of Mexico is using technology to bridge the gap between the present and the future, thus helping Mexico become a full partner in the new economic order heralded by the Information Age.

<table>
<tr><td>7</td><td>**Towards Excellence in Distance Education: National Initiatives in the Canadian Policy Environment**</td></tr>
</table>

7 Towards Excellence in Distance Education: National Initiatives in the Canadian Policy Environment

Judith M. Roberts

Introduction

Canadian researchers, like their colleagues elsewhere, are committed to excellence in distance education and are involved in initiatives examining ways in which to maintain and enhance quality. For example, as professionals working in the country that hosts the Commonwealth of Learning (COL), they are well aware of the COL Working Group on Quality Assurance, co-chaired by Alan Tait (Open University, United Kingdom) and Jocelyn Calvert (Deakin University, Australia). However, they find themselves in a policy environment that is changing quickly. A significant difference is that distance education is receiving considerable attention from government policymakers and the general public. Distance education is no longer seen as peripheral, but as an educational activity that soon will be at the heart of lifelong learning in Canada.

Although education falls under provincial government jurisdiction, according to the Canadian constitution, the federal government is responsible for telecommunications and industrial development. The Hermes satellite program in the 1970s was a prominent instance of the federal government leveraging its telecommunications mandate to affect education (Keough and Roberts 1995). After a period of comparative inactivity in distance education, the federal government and other national agencies are renewing or developing their interest in the application of telecommunications and information technologies to learning and training. This focus is often the result of their mandate in such areas as technology and economic competitiveness, or national testing and curriculum standards.

This paper describes three such national initiatives, suggests some elements common to all of them, and concludes by analyzing their potential implications for distance education research.

Three National Initiatives

Council of Ministers of Education, Canada. The Council of Ministers of Education, Canada (CMEC) was established in 1967 to enable the provincial and territorial ministers of education to consult on matters of mutual interest. It recently published (1995) a review of distance education and open learning in Canada designed to: 1) provide an authoritative description of distance education and open learning in Canada and 2) identify inter-jurisdictional issues that could affect future levels of activity in that field.

The description of Canadian distance education, obtained from data available in the summer/fall of 1994, indicated a number of important facts. First, distance education and open learning activities in Canada continue to expand at all levels. Universities increased their distance education course offerings by 27% from 1990-91 to 1993-94. Sixty-eight percent of community colleges are active in distance education, with an additional 54% of the inactive colleges planning to launch programs soon. Some colleges anticipate growth rates of more than 100%. In the K-12 sector, almost 180,000 public school-level students (both school age and adult) were enrolled in more than 900 distance education courses offered through correspondence schools operated by provincial ministries of education. This figure underestimates distance education activity at the elementary/secondary level, as many schools, school boards, and networks such as Contact North/Contact Nord are involved in distance education. Unfortunately, their activities are not yet tracked and reported for statistical analysis.

Secondly, distance education is reported as being financed differently from on-campus learning. Most postsecondary institutions assign responsibility for distance education to a specialized distance education unit or to a continuing education section. While practice does vary, many of these units collaborate closely with line (academic) departments in the selection of courses and faculty. However, the institutions generally expect distance education and open learning activities to be more self-supporting and less reliant on government funding than are on-campus activities. For example, while 87.9% of colleges' general operating expenses were supported with government funding (1991-92), 47% of responding colleges noted that they receive less than 10% of their distance education funding from provincial government or institutional budgets. The same pattern holds for university campus and distance education funding.

Third, technology usage patterns indicate that substantial changes will have to be made if conversion to Information Highway tools is to be accomplished. At present, multimode technology is the most commonly used medium. Print and telephone are the most frequently used components of multimode, either alone or in combination. Comparatively few institutions are relying on advanced technologies. Research data on the results of their trials are still comparatively rare.

In the second component of the CMEC study, inter-jurisdictional issues were identified through a series of telephone interviews with twenty-one government and institutional representatives in all provinces and territories. Three topics were identified as critical to increased levels of distance education and open learning in Canada: 1) collaboration in the development and accreditation of distance education programs and/or courses, 2) telecommunications across provincial boundaries, and 3) information sharing.

Collaboration in course development and accreditation was seen as vital if learners are to be well served. Interviewees believed that CMEC should focus on common standards and core curriculum elements, leaving customization of peripheral components to individual jurisdictions. They regarded learners' needs as the engine that should drive the education system, and asserted that ministries and institutions were going to "have" to collaborate since the future learner will be highly mobile and will want to take courses and programs from more than one institution, in more than one jurisdiction, at more than one time in their lives. A number of barriers to collaboration were listed, and strategies for overcoming them were suggested.

Employing telecommunications across provincial educational boundaries was seen as inevitable, given aggressive national initiatives by the federal government and private sector. Tariffs, connectivity of equipment, and enhancement of Canadian content were seen as issues that must be addressed if educators are to participate effectively in this new future, rather than being bypassed by other stakeholders.

Information sharing was viewed as essential to avoiding repetition and resource wastage. However, respondents felt that much work remains to be done in defining categories of information that are required, developing viable database business plans, and standardizing definitions and terminology.

CMEC has taken action on each of the three broad issues identified in the interviews. It is developing a manual of best practices in partnerships, which includes successful past and existing joint ventures, as well as those under development. A number of examples of successful partnerships have been forwarded to the CMEC Secretariat by the provinces and territories. A draft document will be circulated to jurisdictions for their comment before the study is published.

CMEC will soon commission a briefing paper related to telecommunications across provincial boundaries to: 1) document federal legislation and international conventions affecting distance education and open learning; 2) describe current regulatory issues from the perspectives of the federal and provincial governments, telecommunications providers, and user groups; and 3) describe the business environment of distance education and open learning.

Alberta Education is working with the CMEC Secretariat to establish a process of sharing information on distance education and open learning among interested partners and stakeholders. One proposal is to establish a clearinghouse that would provide access to a wide range of information on current programs and courses, key contacts involved in developing and delivering programs and courses, and innovations taking place across Canada. It would also create a forum for communication on issues such as policy, regulations and tariffs, telecommunications technology, professional development, employment opportunities, news releases, and other areas of interest and importance. The CMEC is simply acting as a facilitator in this exercise, trying to get all interested partners talking about the possibilities. Preliminary discussions with other stakeholders have begun and additional meetings are planned for the summer and fall of 1995 and beyond.

The Working Group on Learning and Training, Information Highway Advisory Council. In March 1994, Industry Canada appointed a national Information Highway Advisory Council (IHAC), chaired by a former principal of McGill University (Montréal, Québec). IHAC is composed of twenty-nine members from industry, education, research and consumer interests, labor, and other interested communities. All were appointed to a one-year term, which has since been extended to Fall 1995.

IHAC's mandate is to address fifteen public policy issues related to the Information Highway. These issues were grouped into three categories: 1) building a competitive, advanced network infrastructure, 2) content on the Information Highway, and 3) benefits of the Information Highway. This framework was described in some detail in a widely circulated public discussion paper (Industry Canada, April 1994).

Three overriding policy objectives are guiding the council: 1) to create jobs through innovation and investment in Canada, 2) to reinforce Canadian sovereignty and cultural identity, and 3) to ensure universal access at reasonable cost. At the outset, its four operating principles were: 1) an interconnected and interoperable network of networks; 2) collaborative public and private sector development; 3) competition in facilities, products, and services; and 4) privacy protection and network security. At one of its early meetings, the Council adopted a fifth operating principle, as recommended by the Working Group on Learning and Training (one of five working groups), i.e., that lifelong learning be a key design element of the Information Highway.

The Working Group on Learning and Training, co-chaired by a director of education and a labor leader who are members of the Council, is composed of ten people, four of whom are full Council members. They represent the same stakeholder groups as does the Council itself. The Working Group was mandated by the Council to address Issue 14 which has the following focus.

What Consumer Awareness and Learning Opportunities Should be Provided to Enable Canadians to be Effective Users of the Information Highway? The Working Group is developing recommendations for the Council on nine issues which it felt were particularly relevant to Issue 14, i.e., user needs, affordability, learning professions and organizations, Canadian content, access to lifelong learning, management of the negative impacts of technology, market development, protection of intellectual property, and R&D.

The Working Group has met monthly since its appointment. It has engaged a limited number of consultants to assist it in its work and conducted two public consultation processes with learning and training stakeholder groups across the country. While distance education organizations such as the Canadian Association for Distance Education (CADE) and the Open Learning Agency (OLA) of British Columbia have been part of that process, the consultation has gone well beyond "traditional" distance education organizations to include stakeholders such as adult educators, teacher associations, labor, and industry. The Council's report is to be submitted to the Industry Minister in Fall 1995.

Network of Centres of Excellence in Technology-Based Learning. The Networks of Centres of Excellence (NCE) is a federal government program serving all of Canada. Several national research councils that report to the government through Industry Canada administer it. In March 1994, NCE renewed funding of ten existing networks and announced the availability of an additional $48 million to support new networks in five target areas, one of which was technology-based learning. As described in the Competition Announcement (May 1994), a Network of Centres of Excellence in Technology-Based Learning would focus on the application of new and emerging information and communication technologies to education, training, and management/skills development. The Network would also research the social impact, effectiveness, and economies of such applications and work with potential users to apply the research results.

Three applications are now in the final evaluation stage. The three proposals, and the lead institutions in each consortium, are: 1) Canadian Network for Technology-Based Learning: Health-University of Calgary, Alberta; 2)

TeleLearning Network Centres of Excellence-Simon Fraser University, British Columbia; and 3) Technology-Based Learning Network Canada (TBL-CA)-McMaster University, Ontario, and University of Calgary, Alberta.

Implications for Research in Distance Education

Partnerships: Roles and Involvement of the Private Sector. The CMEC and IHAC documents confirm policy trends—identified by Canadian distance education researchers—towards new roles for, and involvement by, the private sector in public education (Keough and Roberts 1995). At the regulatory level, for example, the Canadian Radio-Television and Telecommunications Commission (CTRC) is encouraging competition in the provision of telephone service and following, albeit at a slower pace, the trend in the United States toward deregulation of telecommunications. That these policies are not meeting the needs of distance educators is evidenced by the recent proposal submitted by the Canadian Educational Network Coalition. It suggests that a new, third regulatory category be created for educators. Educational institutions now pay "commercial" rates, the only classification other than "residential" currently available.

In terms of the affordability of new technologies, there is general agreement that the Canadian education market, at whatever level of school, college, or university considered, is potentially large but currently fragmented. CMEC and IHAC both recognize that national courseware development and collaboration across provincial boundaries is necessary to justify the high cost of developing multimedia distance learning programs. They both believe there could be a new role for the private sector in developing learning products for educators.

Canadian researchers have tended to work in an environment in which most of the research content and process (needs identification through evaluation) have been essentially public. Tobin (1995) noted, for example, that Calvert's seminal review of Canadian distance education research did not even include training as a category, presumably because there was no published research on training applications of distance education in the literature she reviewed. Nor did Calvert's review consider private sector research on applications of technology to training. Given the current trends toward private sector involvement, one challenge will be to adjust to whatever role(s) the private sector assumes, and to define how the public sector research community sees itself collaborating with its new entrepreneurial partners. Indeed, some jurisdictions, such as New Brunswick, have explicitly talked of the "learning community" as an industry with public and private components. They view it as an economic sector to be aggressively developed. Canadian distance education researchers have not generally considered the job creation aspects of their work, so this type of economic focus is one that will require adjustment on their part.

Consolidation of Resources. The successful consortium in the NCE competition will become a major focal point for Canadian research in technology-based learning. Since each of the three finalists is a consortium of several stakeholders across Canada, the one ultimately selected should represent a significant concentration of Canadian distance education expertise. There are many obvious strengths to a consortial approach and to the government's focus on collaboration among centers of expertise in all the NCEs. Such advantages include intellectual synergy among research teams, efficiency in resource allocation in a time of financial constraint, minimization of duplication, and facilitation of international collaboration through one point of contact. However, there are also some potential challenges. Perhaps the most serious is the possibility that "all" research funds available will be directed to this new NCE, thus limiting the resources available to researchers who are not part of the consortium and potentially diminishing intellectual diversity.

Pace of Development. The future pace of developments in technology-based learning may well be much faster than that to which researchers have been accustomed. In addition to government interest in the field, there is a strong citizen interest. Two surveys conducted by Gallup Canada for Andersen Consulting have documented that educational services were the most popular of several applications listed for the Information Highway. In the most recent survey (1995), fully 62.6% of those surveyed reported being interested or very interested in educational services. According to the CMEC study, colleges are already experiencing the effect of this public interest in the expanding levels of enrollment being recorded in distance education programs. Stakeholders will hopefully look to research results for guidance, although researchers may need to adjust their agendas to practitioners' demands to move quickly.

Applied Research. The increasing emphasis on re-engineering institutions, businesses, governments, and homes to become learning environments implies that there is potential for large-scale change. One result is that teachers, professors, and trainers are expressing fears of job loss because some administrators are seizing upon technology-based approaches to replace staff and reduce personnel budgets. Two teachers are being replaced by "one teacher and a videoconferencing link." However, distance education research documents that while roles may change in technology-based learning, tutors and other forms of learner support may remain vital to success. The challenge to researchers is to work with administrative and teaching corps to apply the results of their research to large-scale human resource planning. If they do not, the wealth of hard-won knowledge may remain largely unknown outside of the narrow community of distance education researchers and practitioners.

Another result of the trend toward learning environments is that policymakers and administrators are asking for information about the costs and benefits of implementing technology-based approaches to learning and training. Such information is not available except, at best, on a case study basis. To ensure that quality information is available for planning and decision making, researchers may have to develop expertise in the costs and benefits of large-scale approaches to distance education and other applications of technology in learning. Human resource and financial planning thus are two areas in which applied research is becoming a priority.

Conclusion

Should these three initiatives have the hoped for effect, the application of technology-based approaches to learning and training in Canada could increase exponentially. Previous patterns of incremental change will not be valid predictors. Stakeholders are coming to believe that paradigm shifts in learning and training techniques require not only accelerated pilot project activity and research, but also bold vision that addresses teacher fears of job change and loss and administrators' desire to save money.

Distance education researchers have valuable knowledge about how to use technologies to enhance learning. They have the opportunity to positively affect future directions if they will reposition their capabilities, particularly with respect to the implications of their research for human resource and financial planning. With appropriate commitments to quality and integrity, researchers could provide solid human resource scenarios and financial data upon which administrators can base decisions.

Taking such an applied research approach may require that distance education be reconceptualized. Distinctions among the use of stand-alone technology in a classroom, the enrichment of classroom education through conferencing and networking technologies, and the provision of distance education are increasingly academic at the practical level. Nonetheless, the use of terms such as "resource-based learning," "performance-based learning," and "distance education" seem to be "code words" that identify the practitioner as being in the K-12, private, or postsecondary sectors, respectively. If new information highway and technology-based approaches to lifelong learning are seen as different from distance education, and if distance educators are slow to include in their purview a wider range of applications of technology to learning, then opportunities for knowledge transfer based on solid distance education research may be lost. Policymakers and their private sector partners are looking for ways to re-engineer learning and training through the optimal use of technology-based approaches. Distance education researchers may need to extend the application of their research results, and the design of future research activities, so that they become active advocates of best practices in the application of technology to all types of learning.

References

Andersen Consulting. 1995, 1994. *The Information Highway: Gallup Canada. What Canadians think about the Information Highway.* Toronto: Andersen Consulting.

Canada. Council of Ministers of Education (CMEC). 1995. *Distance education and open learning: A report.* Occasional paper No. 1. December. Toronto.

Industry Canada. 1994. *The Canadian Information Highway: Building Canada's Information and Communications Infrastructure.* April, Ottawa: Industry Canada.

Industry Canada. Information Highway Advisory Council (IHAC). 1994. *Canada's Information Highway: Building Canada's information and communications infrastructure. Providing new dimensions for learning, creativity and entrepreneurship.* Progress report of the Information Highway Advisory Council. November, Ottawa: Industry Canada.

Keough, E. M., and J. M. Roberts. 1995. Policy approach for distance and open learning in the information age. In *Why the Information Highway? Lessons From Open and Distance Learning,* eds. J. M. Roberts and E. M. Keough. Toronto: Trifolium Books.

Networks of Centres of Excellence (NCE). 1994. Phase II: Networks of Centres of Excellence: Competition Announcement. May, Ottawa: Networks of Centres of Excellence.

Tobin, J. M. 1995. Evaluation and research frontiers: What do we need to know? In *Why the Information Highway? Lessons from Open and Distance Learning,* eds. J. M. Roberts and E. M. Keough, Toronto: Trifolium Books.

8 Quality Coverage of Higher Education Through Open and Distance Education in Mexico

Alejandro Mungaray

Introduction

Distance education in Mexico has developed in close association with the so-called "open non-scholarized systems." These organizations are intended to use educational programs to provide increased opportunities for individual and social progress in previously underserved geographic and demographic sectors.

The Ministry of Public Education (SEP) created the National Teachers Training Institution in 1947. SEP directed the Institute to give teachers in-service training without interrupting their work. The Institute used a combination of correspondence courses and intensive short courses, given during the teachers' vacation terms. This experience, the first of its type in Latin America, continued until 1975, when the Institute became the General Direction of Teachers Professional Training and Improvement, still under the SEP. It provided the bachelor's degree in Pre-elementary and Elementary Education on an open system basis. This became the model for the open and distance education system of the National Pedagogic University (UPN), established in 1979.

In 1968, the Adult Education Centers, later called Basic Adult Education Centers, were established with the charge to teach courses in literacy and elementary school subjects to persons over fifteen years old. In 1971, the televised secondary school was created, which efficiently corrected the lack of schools and teachers in the countryside.

Enrollment at all levels grew at a significant rate during the 1970s. This demographic phenomenon coincided with the great efforts to promote open education programs in Mexico. In 1971, a presidential decree mandated the founding of the Center for the Study of Advanced Education Means and Procedures (CEMPAE). CEMPAE developed the educational technology that served as a basis for implementing intensive adult elementary schools (1974), open secondary schools (1976), and open high schools (1979). The lack of attention to matters of basic education led to the creation of the National Adult Education Institution (INEA) in 1982.

Beginning in 1976, SEP developed—at the high school level—the open systems of the Bachelors College and the General Direction of Industrial-Technological Education. At the postsecondary level, the National Autonomous University of Mexico (UNAM) established the Open University System (SUA) and the National Polytechnic Institute (IPN) in 1972. The General Direction of Technological Institutes (DGIT) of the SEP introduced higher education programs in 1974, with the Open Teaching System (SEA) and the Open Technological System, respectively.

The number of public and private institutions and agencies offering educational services via open and distance systems, at both the high school and postsecondary levels, has increased significantly. However, because of the diversity of schemes within these levels, open and distance education has developed heterogeneously. The Federal Government has had to take actions to coordinate and orient these efforts; to this end it created the Open Systems Coordinating Board. Before 1984, SEP's General Director of Educative Evaluation had the task of providing continuity to Coordinating Board actions.

The Coordinating Board convened the first two national meetings on open education in 1987 and 1988. Due to administrative changes, the third meeting did not take place until 1991. The organizers called the 1991 meeting in order to reestablish interinstitutional coordination, promote exchanges of experiences among the participants, and develop plans for action. This meeting resulted in the creation of the Interinstitutional and Interdisciplinary Commission on Open and Distance Education (CIIEAD), the function of which is to serve as a liaison between the educational institutions, university associations, and government agencies involved in this teaching modality.

Open and Distance Education in Mexico

In 1995, CIIEAD listed twenty-six high school-level institutions with open and distance programs, and nineteen at the postsecondary level. In the former, academic and administrative structures reflect a strong attachment to traditional methods. Forty percent continue to require selection examinations, and counseling is mandatory in 50%; both practices reflect a high degree of formality. In the postsecondary institutions, it is interesting to note that in academic years 1993-1994 and 1994-1995, students attending through open and distance education schemes represented from 3.9% to 10.2% of their total enrollment.

Among the public institutions developing open and distance education programs at both undergraduate and graduate degree levels, the following are the most prominent: the UNAM with ten schools, the UPN with seventy units, the IPN, the Veracruzan University (UV), the University of Guadalajara (UdeG), the University of Colima (UC), and the DGIT of the SEP, with its thirty centers. In the private sector, the Technological and Higher Studies Institute of Monterrey (ITESM), the Educative Communication Latin American Institute (ILCE), the University of Monterrey (UDEM), the Banking and Commercial School (EBC), the Panamerican Institute (UP), and the University of the Atemajac Valley (UNIVA) lead the field.

Of the strictly undergraduate institutions, the UP of Nuevo Laredo enrolls 10.2% of its total student body through the distance education modality, followed by the Veracruzan University, at 9.7%. In the teachers schools system, the UPN tallies 97.1% of its enrollment via open and distance education; at the graduate level the ITESM enrolls 9%.

Of the nineteen institutions with open and distance programs at the postsecondary level, five offer them nationwide, five on a regional level, seven at the state level, and two at the local level (SEP 1992, 30). The organizational models are of a heterogeneous nature, from those that promote an independent quality of learning to those that are highly restrictive, requiring admission examinations, counseling, and serialization of courses. Most, however, take an intermediate position. Only four offer transmission via satellite. However, half support their courses with computer equipment, in addition to printed materials, video, audio, telephone, and fax.

Graduate programs are stepping up their use of telecommunications networks. This is most pronounced in master's-level programs taught by the ITESM and the ICLE. In addition, the Veterinary Medicine and Zootechnics school of the UNAM is using distance tutorial programs (Pallán, et. al. 1944, 32). Printed materials clearly predominate, followed by audiovisual and computer resources, and—in one case—satellite.

While the development of the electronic distance education modality began in the early 1970s, its importance and viability have been growing rapidly in recent years, particularly since the development of individual computers linked into networks that can provide data, voice, and image transmission. The flexibility inherent in such systems allows them to take advantage of self-teaching. Networks permit self-instruction according to the potential of each individual, without regard to his or her age and social position. This has permitted a sizable number of persons in Mexico (though still not in proportion to countries with a higher degree of economic and social development) to continue with their professional or cultural preparation, according to their individual circumstances and interests.

Although it is true that in some cases open and distance education programs turn out to be remedial adaptations of conventional systems, it is also true that they have provided some real opportunities for innovation. These programs have permitted the development of flexible organizations, the application of modern communication technologies, the accreditation of knowledge obtained in partnership with the commercial and industrial sectors, the development of standardized professional profiles, and the growth of graduate-level faculty. The media of distance education permit innovation based on the use of simulations, videos, animations, and other elements not used in traditional classes. It also includes the use of interactive systems through center link-ups. Courses can be given at undergraduate, graduate, and on-going education levels. This combination of media favors responsible, innovative, and flexible instruction in which the student is linked to the school by means of a tutor or via the interinstitutional academic network (OLA 1994).

Distance education through data processing and academic computing networks is opening up possibilities for the formation of additional networks via satellite or more unconventional modalities. To the extent this potential is developed, the factors currently limiting coverage could soon become things of the past. Through technological and organizational innovation, education of the highest quality can be made available to large segments of the population (Jones 1991, 32).

Conditions for Innovation in Higher Education through Open and Distance Education

The government and the higher education institutions believe that recent advances in quality assessment techniques are critical. However, they also believe that the higher education system requires organizational changes in order to meet major challenges in productive and social development. Higher education institutions must provide opportunities for lifelong education in the face of constant changes in the economy and within the professions. This is the first challenge.

The second challenge concerns the need for institutions to broaden their distance education enrollment beyond their current fourteen percent of the total, without relinquishing their quality standards. Such challenges necessitate far-reaching organizational and directional changes. Like other social institutions that supply goods to the public, colleges and universities must first commit themselves to promote the well being of society, then act on that commitment (Stevens 1993).

Data Processing and Telecommunications

Information and coordination are critical to the success of all organizational initiatives. The information age, based on computers and their interconnecting networks, is having a substantial impact within organizations, particularly the larger ones in which many employees interact. Such organizations need flexibility in order to deal with complicated internal response processes and the growing variety of demands placed on them.

Access to information is essential in academic and scientific work. Data processing networks are improving communications among university researchers, providing access to remote resources, and facilitating distance education and personalized learning (Daltabuit 1994, 4-5). As noted above, a sizable number of Mexican educational institutions are availing themselves of technological resources in order to optimize their human and material resources and to encourage this trend in other institutions. Thus, in addition to technological and organizational innovations, educational institutions have developed new data processing networks to supplement instructional efforts. The faculty preparation program designed by the ITESM and the University of Coahuila provides a good example.

The most important public networks in Mexico are the REDUNAM and those operated by the IPN, CONACYT, MEXNET, and RUTYC. Generally an institution can be connected to one or several of them. Even though connections to these networks are used mainly to access foreign data banks, it is also clear that the national information systems are now becoming important to both Mexican and international users. As investment resources increase in the future, the possibilities for innovation can be even greater, allowing for reconversion of the national data banks. Progress in the preparation of qualified human resources will also facilitate such developments.

The National Backbone Network was recently integrated into the core of the Public Universities and Institutional Council of the ANUIES as a users consortium, empowered to subcontract network operations and management to third parties. Interconnecting the higher education institutions as soon as possible, at the lowest cost and with maximum services, is critically important to our country. This will position Mexico to take large qualitative leaps in matters of academic cooperation.

The Organization of University Networks

An environment of organizational innovation has been gaining ground in Mexico, giving direction to the demands of academics that they be allowed greater involvement in all matters related to quality improvement. On the one hand, many schools are initiating important **institutional decentralization** processes in order to more thoroughly cover regional needs via a decentralized campus. On the other hand, **interinstitutional networks of academics** have proliferated according to disciplinary and interdisciplinary interests (Pallán 1995a, 26). These networks are important because they have promoted a wide mobility of faculty and students among the different regions and institutes. In addition, they are laying the groundwork to strengthen the organization of distance education through tutelage and research, with a higher participation of academics interested in cooperating along both disciplinary and interdisciplinary lines.

The organizational and structural trends now dominating higher education institutions—decentralization and interinstitutional networks—are promoting new, high-quality answers to the need for a productive environment. Along this route of organizational change and technological innovation lie great possibilities for improving the quality of educational institutions' resources, teachers, and students. The National Pacific Rim Researchers Network is focused on this objective, as are the researchers from state universities located on the Pacific coast, who have instituted a Master's Program in International Relations offered on an open and distance basis (Rivas 1993).

It is particularly significant that the interinstitutional networks of academics are beginning to create programs offered through open and distance formats. This enables university professional schools to respond more successfully to the needs of the commercial and manufacturing sectors, as well as to students' and young professionals' expectations of social mobility. This is creating challenges to the traditional attitudes of both educational institutions and business and industry. Both can share the on-going preparation and updating of professionals and encourage their personnel to learn from each other (Nohria 1992).

Perspective and Pertinence of Open and Distance Education

The outlook for open and distance education in Mexico is better than ever, especially as a means of meeting the major challenges of higher education. These challenges include: 1) promoting individual improvement and social mobility, 2) preparing higher quality teachers at all levels through graduate studies, and 3) training and retraining personnel to meet the needs of business and industry.

With regard to social mobility, it is important to note that the discrepancies in education levels in Mexico are substantial. While the higher education systems of the United States and Canada serve about 70% of the population in the appropriate age groups, in Mexico the figure is only 14%. Further, the prevailing academic organizational schemes and the size of the infrastructure do not appear sufficient to permit satisfactory short-term responses.

Concerning the preparation of faculty, the multiple efforts thus far in Mexican higher education have yet to result in a postgraduate degree devoted to teaching and research. For the sake of comparison, while in 1993 only 3% of the total faculty personnel held a doctor's degree, in the United States the percentage stood at 55% (Pallán 1995b). Open and distance education offers possibilities for much more rapid advancement in preparing candidates for postgraduate studies in higher education. With the introduction of an appropriate organizational structure and a sound follow-up system, targeted quality levels should not be negatively affected.

The difficult relationship between higher education institutions and the private sector in matters of training and retraining (Mungaray 1992) can surely improve through a joint effort to develop distance education. The possibilities of learning from each other should increase with currently proposed professional service requirements. Joint accountability and enthusiastic participation can do a great deal to build a new era of social relations between the public and private sectors.

References

Interinstitutional and Interdisciplinary Commission of Open and Distance Education 40–41, (CIIEAD) 1995. January 30, March 13.

Daltabuit, E. 1994. *National Academic Network.* Available and Desirable Services, Mimco.

Jones, G. R. 1991. *Make all America a School.* Englewood: Mind Extension University.

Mungaray, A. 1992. Requirements for skill, training and retraining in the Mexican food and drink industry. *Journal of International Food and Agribusiness Marketing* 4(1):71–93.

Nohria N. 1992. Is a network perspective a useful way of studying organizations? In *Networks and Organizations. Structure, Form and Action,* eds. N. Nohria and R. G. Eccles, 1–22. Boston, MA: Harvard Business School Press.

Open Learning Agency (OLA). *Annual Report 1993-94*. British Columbia, Canada.

Pallán, C. et. al. 1994. Higher education in Mexico. *Today's Issues in Higher Education* (Mexico) (1):102.

Pallán, C. 1995a. Growth, evaluation and innovations in higher education (1988-1994). *Public Administration Magazine* (Mexico) (89):1–35.

Pallán, C. 1995b. The social challenges of Mexican higher education and international cooperation. Paper presented in the panel, International Dimension of Higher Education, February 28, Autonomous University of Guadalajara, Guadalajara, Mexico.

Rivas, F. 1993 The construction of a subject of study: The case of the Pacific Rim. *Higher Education Magazine* 4(88):69–79.

SEP 1992. Open and Distance Education in Mexico. Mexico: Interinstitutional and Interdisciplinary Open and Distance Education Commission.

Stevens, J. B. 1993. *The Economics of Collective Choice*. Boulder, CO: Westview Press.

The author would like to thank Hilario Aguilar, Graciela Dìaz and Clara Gallardo for their valuable support and comments. All are members of the working group on distance education in ANUIES (Academic Secretary of the National Association of Universities and Higher Education Institutions of Mexico).

9   The Transformation of Distance Education to Distributed Learning

Christopher J. Dede

Introduction

The development of high performance computing and communications is creating new media, such as the WorldWide Web and virtual realities. In turn, these new media enable new types of messages and experiences; for example, interpersonal interactions in immersive, synthetic environments lead to the formation of virtual communities. The innovative kinds of pedagogy empowered by these emerging media, messages, and experiences make possible a transformation of conventional distance education—which replicates traditional classroom teaching across barriers of distance and time—into an alternative instructional paradigm: distributed learning.

Implications of New Media for Distance Education

What does the evolution of new media mean for distance educators? A medium is in part a channel for conveying content; new media like the Internet mean that we can readily reach wider, more diverse audiences. Just as important, however, is that a medium is a representational container enabling new types of messages (e.g., sometimes a picture is worth a thousand words). Since the process of thinking is based on representations such as language and imagery, the process of learning is strongly shaped by the types of instructional messages we can exchange with students. Emerging representational containers, such as hypermedia, enable a broader, more powerful repertoire of pedagogical strategies.

The global marketplace and the communications and entertainment industries are driving the rapid evolution of high performance computing and communications. Regional, national, and global "information infrastructures" that enhance our abilities to sense and act and learn across barriers of distance and time are developing. The ways in which information is created, delivered, and used in business, government, and society are swiftly changing. To successfully prepare students to become workers and citizens, educators must incorporate into the curriculum experiences in creating and utilizing new forms of expression, such as multimedia. Information infrastructures offer channels for delivering such technology-intensive learning experiences just-in-time, anyplace, and on-demand (Dede 1994).

The "information superhighway" metaphor now widely used to convey the implications of high performance computing and communications is inadequate. Such an analogy is the equivalent of someone declaring in 1895 that the airplane will be the canal system of the 20th century. Backward looking metaphors focus on what we can automate—how we can use new channels to send conventional forms of content more efficiently—but miss the true innovation: redefining how we communicate and educate through the use of new types of messages and experiences in order to be more effective. Since emerging forms of representation such as hypermedia and virtual reality are in their early stages of development, we are just beginning to understand how they shape not only their messages, but also their users.

Many people are still reeling from the first impact of high performance computing and communications: shifting from the challenge of not getting enough information to the challenge of surviving too much information. The core skill for today's workplace is not foraging for data, but filtering a plethora of incoming information. The emerging literacy we all must master requires diving into a sea of information and immersing ourselves in data to harvest patterns of knowledge, just as fish extract oxygen from water via their gills. Understanding how to structure learning experiences to make such immersion possible is the core of the new rhetoric of educators. Expanding traditional definitions of literacy and rhetoric into immersion-centered experiences of interacting with information is crucial to preparing students for full participation in 21st century society (Dede 1992).

Conventional distance education is similar to traditional classroom instruction, save that it uses technology-based delivery systems. In contrast, emerging forms of distributed learning are reconceptualizing education's mission, clients, process, and content; this new instructional paradigm is based both on shifts in what learners need to be prepared for the future and on new capabilities in the pedagogical repertoire of teachers. Four new forms of expression are shaping the emergence of distributed learning as a new pedagogical model:

- knowledge webs complement teachers, texts, libraries, and archives as sources of information,

- interactions in virtual communities complement face-to-face relationships in classrooms,
- experiences in synthetic environments extend learning-by-doing in real world settings, and
- sensory immersion helps learners grasp reality through illusion.

We are just beginning to understand how these representational containers can reshape the content, process, and delivery of conventional distance education. Information infrastructures are the lever for this evolution, just as the steam engine was the driver for the industrial revolution.

Knowledge Webs

"Knowledge webs" enable distributed access to experts, archival resources, authentic environments, and shared investigations. We are accustomed to asking a well-informed person in our immediate vicinity for guidance, to consulting printed information or watching a news program, to visiting exhibits (such as a zoo) to learn about different types of environments, and to conducting informal experiments to understand how reality works. Often, these information gathering and creation activities are constrained by barriers of distance, restricted access, scheduling difficulties, and the limits of one's personal expertise in investigation.

Educators and students can join distributed conferences that provide an instant network of contacts with useful skills, a personal brain trust with just-in-time answers to immediate questions via information infrastructures. In time, these informal sources of expertise will utilize embedded "groupware" tools to enhance collaboration. On the Internet, on-line archival resources are increasingly linked into the WorldWide Web, accessible through "webcrawlers" such as Mosaic and Netscape. Eventually, artificial intelligence-based guides will facilitate navigating through huge amounts of stored information.

Virtual exhibits that duplicate real-world settings (e.g., museums) are emerging; these environments make possible a wide variety of experiences without the necessity of travel or scheduling. Distributed science projects enable conducting shared experiments dispersed across time and space, each team member learning more than would be possible in isolation about the phenomenon being studied and about scientific investigation. Combined, all these capabilities to enhance information gathering and creation form knowledge webs.

However, access to data does not automatically expand students' knowledge; the availability of information does not intrinsically create an internal framework of ideas learners can use to interpret reality. While presentational approaches transmit material rapidly from source to student, this content often evaporates quickly from learners' minds. To be motivated to master concepts and skills, students need to see how what they are learning is connected to the rest of their lives and to the mental models they already use. Even when learners are drilled in a topic until facts are indefinitely retained—we all know that the sum of a triangle's internal angles is 180 degrees—this knowledge is often "inert"; most people do not know how to apply the abstract principles they memorized in school to solving real-world problems. To move students beyond assimilating inert facts into generating better mental models, teachers must structure learning experiences that highlight how new ideas can provide insights in intriguing, challenging situations.

The curriculum is already overcrowded with low-level information; teachers frantically race through required material, helping students memorize factual data to be regurgitated on mandated, standardized tests. Using information infrastructures as a fire hose to spray yet more information into educational settings would make this situation even worse. Without skilled facilitation, many learners who access current knowledge webs will flounder in a morass of unstructured data (Dede and Palumbo 1990).

A vital, emerging form of literacy for educators to communicate is the means of transforming archival information into personal knowledge. However, moving students from access, through assimilation, to appropriation requires educational experiences that promote knowledge construction by unsophisticated learners and that help them make sense of massive, incomplete, and inconsistent information sources. Weaving learner-centered, constructivist usage of linked, on-line materials into the curriculum and culture of traditional educational institutions is one of the next stages of evolution for conventional distance education.

Virtual Communities

Virtual communities that provide support from people who share common joys and trials offer a second capability for enhancing distributed learning. We are accustomed to face-to-face interaction as a means of getting to know people, sharing ideas and experiences, enjoying others' humor and fellowship, and finding solace. In a different manner, distributed learning via information infrastructures can satisfy these needs at any time, any place. Some people (shy, reflective, comfortable with emotional distance) even find asynchronous, low bandwidth communication more "authentic" than face-to-face verbal exchange. They can take time before replying in order to compose a more elegant message, as well as to refine the emotional nuances they wish to convey. This alternative conception of authenticity may reflect a dimension to learning styles different from the visual, auditory, symbolic, and kinesthetic differentiations now used.

To dramatically improve learning outcomes by evolving to new pedagogical strategies, distance educators need the virtual communities that information infrastructures make possible. Learning is social as well as intellectual. Individual, isolated attempts to make sense of complex data can easily fail unless the learner is encouraged by some larger group that is constructing shared knowledge. In addition, institutional evolution is a communal enterprise; educational innovators need emotional and intellectual support from others who have similar challenges in their lives.

Moreover, formal education comprises only 19% of students' time. No matter how well schooling is done, achieving major gains in learning requires that the other 81% of pupils' lives be educationally fulfilling as well. This necessitates close cooperation and shared responsibility for distributed learning among society's educational agents (families, social service agencies, workplaces, mass media, schools, higher education), which virtual communities can enhance. For example, involving families more deeply in their children's education may be the single most powerful lever for improved learning outcomes. Virtual parent-teacher conferences and less formal social interchanges make such involvement more likely for parents who will never come to a PTA meeting or a school-based event. In many regions across the U.S., community networks are emerging that, among other missions, enhance education by enabling distributed discourse among all the stakeholders in quality schooling.

Another illustration of a distributed learning use for virtual communities is peer tutoring. This instructional approach aids all students involved, both intellectually and emotionally, but is difficult to implement in traditional classroom settings. Outside of school, virtual interactions enhanced by groupware tools readily enable such student-student relationships, as well as preparing their participants for later use of distributed problem-solving techniques in adult workplace settings. Telementoring and teleapprenticeships between students and workplace experts are similar examples of applying virtual community capabilities to distributed learning.

Creating a sense of communion among a distributed group linked by low to moderate bandwidth networking is a complex challenge. Some people favor technology-mediated communication as their most authentic way of sharing ideas and enjoying fellowship. Most people prefer face-to-face interaction, but find the convenience of just-in-time, anyplace access to others often outweighs the disadvantages of distributed sharing of ideas, experiences, and support. Groupware tools, a capable moderator, and shared interactivity and control are important for sustaining the vitality of virtual communities, as is occasional direct contact among participants.

To succeed, distributed learning must balance virtual and direct interaction in sustaining communion among people. A relationship based only on telephone conversation lacks the vibrancy that face-to-face interchange provides. Similarly, while digital video will broaden the bandwidth of virtual interactions on information infrastructures, teleconferencing will never completely substitute for direct personal contact. We can expect a variety of social inventions that provide the best of both worlds to emerge; for example, national professional conferences may sponsor pre- and post-conference virtual communities that enable participants to make the most of the limited face-to-face time they have. Through their expertise in encouraging interactivity across disparate geographic locations, distance educators have important insights to contribute in the evolution of virtual communities.

Shared Synthetic Environments that Complement Real World Experiences

Another emerging capability for enhancing distributed learning is shared synthetic environments that extend our experiences beyond what we can encounter in the real world. Information infrastructures are not only channels for transmitting content, but also communal virtual worlds that students can enter and explore. Just as single-user simulations allow an individual to interact with a model of reality (e.g., flying a virtual airplane), distributed simulations enable many people at different locations to inhabit and shape a common synthetic environment. For example, the U.S. Department of Defense uses distributed simulation technology to create virtual battlefields on which learners at remote sites develop collective military skills. The appearance and capabilities of graphically represented military equipment alter second-by-second as the virtual battle evolves ("dial-a-war").

Distributed simulation is a representational container that can empower a broad range of educational uses (e.g., virtual factories, hospitals, cities). The vignette below depicts a hypothetical future application that promotes distributed learning outside the classroom through "edutainment."

Edutainment in Cyberspace

Roger was unobtrusively sidling across the Bridge of the Starship Enterprise when the Captain spotted him out of the corner of his eye. "Take the helm, Ensign Pulver," growled Captain Jean-Luc Picard, "and pilot a course through the corona of that star at lightspeed 0.999. We have astrophysical samples to collect. You'll have to guard against strange relativistic effects at that speed, but our shields cannot stand the radiation flux we would experience through traveling less quickly." Roger had intended to sneak onto the Ecology Deck of the Starship and put in a little work on his biology class project in controlling closed-system pollution levels, but no such luck. Worse yet, he suspected that the Vulcan communications officer watching him while she translated a message in French was in fact the "avatar" (computer-graphics representation of a person) of a woman he admired who sat three rows behind him in his languages class. Of course, he could be wrong; she might be someone teleporting into this simulation from who knows where or could even be a "knowbot" (a machine-based simulated personality used to simplify the job of instructors directing an instructional simulation).

Buying a little time by summoning up the flight log, Roger glanced curiously around the bridge to see what new artifacts his fellow students had added since yesterday to this MUD (Multi-User-Dungeon or Dimension, a current type of adventure game in which participants mutually evolve an elaborate, shared synthetic environment by continuously modifying its contents). In one corner, an intriguing creature was sitting in a transparent box, breathing a bluish-green atmosphere—maybe this was the long-awaited alien the anthropology and biology majors were creating as a mutual project. The 3-D goggles from his Nintendo++ set intensified the illusion that the lizard-like countenance was staring right at him.

"Impulse Engines to full speed, Mister," barked Captain Picard! "This Mage (human expert guiding the evolution of a virtual environment) seems rather grumpy for a regular teacher," thought Roger, "maybe he's a visiting fireman from the new Net-the-Experts program." On his Console, Roger rapidly selected equations that he hoped would yield the appropriate relativistic corrections for successfully navigating through the star's corona. He hoped to impress Captain Picard as a means of improving his chances for promotion. Last week's setback, getting motion sick while "riding" on a virtual gas molecule that was illustrating Brownian motion, had not helped his chances...

This vignette shows how education could be situated in a synthetic universe analogous to a authentic real-world environment, but more intriguing. Moreover, such a distributed learning strategy leverages a huge installed base of sophisticated information technology—home videogame consoles—as well as the substantial motivation inculcated by the entertainment industry.

Even without the added enhancement of visual imagery, the rise on the Internet of text-based shared synthetic environments (e.g., MUDs, MUSEs, MOOs) illustrates people's fascination with participatory virtual worlds. The continual evolution of distributed simulations based on participants' collaborative interactions keeps these shared virtual environments from becoming boring and stale. In contrast to standard adventure games, in which you wander through someone else's fantasy, the ability to personalize an environment and receive recognition from others for adding to the shared context is attractive to many people. Part of why we read fiction or watch dramatic productions is to escape the ordinary in a manner that increases our insights or refreshes us to plunge back into real-world challenges. Shared virtual experiences on the National Information Infrastructure (NII) can complement books, plays, television, movies, and concerts in their ability to take us beyond the daily grind—the challenge is to move past escapism into metaphorical comprehension and catharthis (Dede, in press).

Sensory Immersion to Grasp Reality Through Illusion

In addition to distributed simulation, advances in high performance computing and communications also are enabling learners' sensory immersion in "artificial realities." Via an immersion interface based on computerized clothing and a head-mounted display, the participant feels "inside" an artificial reality rather than viewing a synthetic environment through a computer monitor's screen; virtual reality is analogous to diving rather than looking into an aquarium window. Using sensory immersion to present abstract, symbolic data in tangible form is a powerful means of attaining insights into real world phenomena (Dede 1993b).

For example, "visualization" is an emerging type of rhetoric that enhances learning by using the human visual system to find patterns in large amounts of information. People have very powerful pattern recognition capabilities for images; much of our brain is "wetware" dedicated to this purpose. As a result, when tabular data of numerical variables such as temperature, pressure, and velocity are transfigured into graphical objects whose shifts in shape, texture, size, color, and motion convey their changing values, increased insights are often attained. For example, graphical data visualizations that model thunderstorm-related phenomena (e.g., downbursts, air flows, cloud movements) are valuable in helping meteorologists and students understand the dynamics of these weather systems.

As information infrastructures increasingly enable people to access large databases without regard to distance, visualization tools can expand human perceptions so that we recognize underlying relationships that would otherwise be swamped in a sea of numbers. One good way to enhance creativity is to make the familiar strange and the strange, familiar; adding sonification and even tactile sensations to visual imagery can make abstract things tangible and vice versa. For example, expanding human perceptions (e.g. allowing a medical student—like Superman—to see the human body through X-ray vision) is a powerful method for deepening learners' motivation and their intuitions about physical phenomena. My current research centers on assessing the potential value of sensory immersion and synthetic environments for learning material as disparate as electromagnetic fields and intercultural sensitivities (Salzman, Dede, and Loftin, in press).

The vignette below illustrates how sensory immersion might someday be combined with knowledge webs, virtual collaboration, and synthetic environments to enable powerful forms of distributed learning.

81

Collaborative Training in a Shared Synthetic Environment

Karen sat down at her educational workstation, currently configured as an electronics diagnosis/repair training device. When sign-in was complete, the workstation acknowledged her readiness to begin Lesson Twelve: Teamed Correction of Malfunctioning Communications Sensor. Her "knowbot" (machine-based agent) established a telecommunications link to Phil, her partner in the exercise, who was sitting at a similar device in his home thirty miles away. "Why did I have the bad luck to get paired with this clown?" she thought, noting a hung-over expression on his face in the video window. "He probably spent last night partying instead of preparing for the lesson." A favorite saying of the problem solving expert to whom she was apprenticed flitted through her mind, "The effectiveness of computer-supported cooperative work can be severely limited by the team's weakest member."

"Let's begin," Karen said decisively. "I'll put on the DataArm to find and remove the faulty component. You use the CT (cognitive transducer) to locate the appropriate repair procedure." Without giving him time to reply, she put on her head-mounted display, brought up an AR (artificial reality) depicting the interior of a TransStar communications groundstation receiver, and began strapping on the DataArm. The reality-engine's meshing of computer graphics and video images presented a near-perfect simulation, although too rapid movements could cause objects to blur slightly. Slowly, she "grasped" a microwrench with her "hand" on the screen and began to loosen the first fastener on the amplifier's cover. Haptic feedback from the DataArm to her hand completed the illusion, and she winced as she realized the bolt was rusty and would require care to remove without breaking.

Meanwhile, Phil called up the CT for Electronics Repair; on the screen, a multicolored, three-dimensional network of interconnections appeared and began slowly rotating. He groaned; just looking at the knowledge web made his eyes hurt. Since the screen resolution was excellent, he suspected that last night's fourth margarita was the culprit. Phil said slowly, "Lesson Twelve," and a trail was highlighted in the network. He began to skim through a sea of stories, harvesting metaphors and analogies, while simultaneously monitoring a small window in the upper left-hand corner of the screen that was beginning to fill with data from the diagnostic sensors on Karen's DataArm.

Several paragraphs of text were displayed at the bottom of the screen, ignored by Phil. Since his learning style is predominantly visual and auditory rather than symbolic, he listened to the web as it vocalizes this textual material, watching a graphical pointer maneuver over a blueprint. Three figurines are gesturing near the top of the display, indicating that they know related stories. On the right hand side of the monitor, an interest-based browser shows index entries grouped by issue, hardware configuration, and functional system.

Traversing the network at the speed with which Karen was working was difficult, given his hangover, and he made several missteps. "Knowledge Base," Phil said slowly, "infer what the optical memory chip does to the three-dimensional quantum well superlattice." The voice of his knowbot suddenly responded, "You seem to be assuming a sensor flaw when the amplifier may be the problem."

"Shut up!" Phil thought savagely, hitting the cut-off switch. He groaned when he visualized his knowbot feeding the cognitive audit trail of his actions into the workstations of his trainer and the corporation's communications repair expert; he could not terminate those incriminating records. Phil cringed when he imagined his trainer's "avatar" giving him another lecture on his shortcomings. Mentally, he began phrasing an elaborate excuse to send his instructors via email at the termination of the lesson.

Meanwhile, Karen was exasperatedly watching the window on her AR display in which Phil's diagnostic responses should have been appearing. "He's hopeless," she thought. Her knowbot's "consciousness sensor" (a biofeedback link that monitors user attention and mood) interrupted with a warning: "Your blood pressure is rising rapidly; this could trigger a migraine headache." "Why," Karen said sadly, "couldn't I have lived in the age when students learned from textbooks..."

Young people like magical alternate realities; and the entertainment industry profits by providing amusement parks, videogames, movies, and television programs that build on this fascination. Distance educators too can profit, in a different way, by building eerily beautiful environments for sensory immersion that arouse curiosity and empower shared fantasy, leading to guided inquiry. If we forswear distributed learning based on mystery, intrigue, and "edutainment," we risk losing the generation growing up with high-performance computing and communications to the mindless mercies of videogames.

Assessing the Impact of Distributed Learning on Conventional Schooling

The distributed learning vignettes depicted above may seem financially implausible; where will schools, colleges, and universities find the resources to implement these alternative pedagogical models? An analogy can be drawn to the early-1980s competition among cable TV vendors to receive exclusive franchises from communities. Those educators smart enough to participate in that bargaining process received substantial resources—buildings wired for free, dedicated channels, sophisticated production equipment—because the vendors knew public service applications would help determine who won. In the same manner, during today's much larger war in the information services industry, distance educators who have innovative alternatives to "talking heads" instruction can find vendors happy to share the costs in exchange for help with the regulators, legislators, and judges who are determining which coalitions will manage the nation's information infrastructures.

However, as with business, the evolution of technology creates new markets and expanded competitors for schools and colleges. As one illustration, prestigious universities may develop nationwide offerings of standard courses (e.g., PSYC 101) taught by telegenic, internationally recognized authorities. In such a strategy, high production-value presentations would be coupled with frequent, interactive teleconferences; mentoring via electronic mail; and occasional face-to-face meetings of locally enrolled students led by a practitioner. This approach would not intrigue learners interested in a residential college experience, but could be very attractive to students at commuter campuses. With sufficient economies of scale, this delivery method would have lower costs than our present system of similar standard courses duplicated at every institution. While many faculty would disparage this type of instruction, state legislatures could easily see such a model as an attractive way to cut their expenditures for higher education—a method applicable to every course for which a substantial textbook market exists.

In such an evolution of distance education, colleges and universities would be reshaped as profoundly as American business has been altered by technologies enabling the global marketplace. Given their responsibilities for socialization and custodial protection, public schools would be less affected by the erosion of geographic monopolies through distributed learning technologies. However, the home schooling and educational voucher movements see information infrastructures as an attractive alternative means of instructional delivery. If distributed learning is not incorporated into public schools' classrooms, teachers may find a decade from now that they have a smaller fraction of students enrolled and fewer taxpayers willing to provide funding.

Transforming Distance Education to Distributed Learning

Today, distance education is primarily used in selective situations to overcome problems of scale (not enough students in a single location) and rarity (a specialized subject not locally available). Such instruction is often seen as "half a loaf" pedagogy; better than nothing, but not as good as face-to-face teaching. However, the global marketplace and emerging information infrastructures are changing this situation. Educators must help all students become adept at distanced interaction, for skills of information gathering from remote sources and collaboration with dispersed team members are as central to the future American workplace as learning to perform structured tasks quickly was to the industrial revolution. Also, by increasing the diversity of human resources available to students, distributed learning can enhance equity—as well as pluralism—to prepare for competition in the world marketplace. Virtual classrooms have a wider spectrum of peers with whom learners can collaborate than any local region can offer, and a broader range of teachers and mentors than any single educational institution can afford.

In a few years, high performance computing and communications will make knowledge utilities, virtual communities, shared synthetic environments, and sensory immersion as routine a part of everyday existence as the telephone, television, radio, and newspaper are today. Distributed learning experiences will be seen as vital for all learners even when the same content could be taught face-to-face, and all teaching will have some attributes of "distance education" (Dede 1993a). Keeping a balance between virtual interaction and direct interchange will be important, however. Technology-mediated communication and experience supplement, but do not replace, immediate involvement in real settings.

High performance computing and communications won't be a "silver bullet" that magically solves all problems of education; thoughtful and caring participation is vital for making these new capabilities truly valuable. Even then, at times a sloppy, handwritten note delivered through surface mail will mean more to the recipient than an instantly transmitted, elegantly formatted electronic message. New media complement existing approaches to widen our repertoire of communication; properly designed, they need not eliminate choices or force us into high tech, low touch situations.

How a medium shapes its users, as well as its message, is a central issue in understanding the transformation of distance education into distributed learning. The telephone creates conversationalists; the book develops imaginers, who can conjure a rich mental image from sparse symbols on a printed page. Much of television programming induces passive observers; other shows, such as Sesame Street and public affairs programs, can spark users' enthusiasm and enrich their perspectives. As we move beyond naive "superhighway" concepts to see the true potential impact of information infrastructures, society will face powerful new interactive media capable of great good or ill. Today's "couch potatoes," vicariously living in the fantasy world of television, could become tomorrow's "couch funguses," immersed as protagonists in 3-D soap operas while the real world deteriorates. The most significant influence on the evolution of distance education will not be the technical development of more powerful devices, but the professional development of wise designers, educators, and learners.

References

Dede, C. In press. The evolution of constructivist learning environments: Immersion in distributed, virtual worlds. *Educational Technology*.

Dede, C. 1994. *Technologies Driving the National Information Infrastructure: Policy Implications for Distance Education.* Los Alamitos, CA: Southwest Regional Educational Laboratory.

Dede, C. 1993a. Beyond distributed multimedia: A virtual forum for learning. *ED Journal* 7 September:14–18.

Dede, C. 1993b. Evolving from multimedia to virtual reality. In *Educational Multimedia and Hypermedia Annual,* ed. H. Maurer, 123–130. Charlottesville, VA: Association for the Advancement of Computing in Education.

Dede, C. 1992. Education in the 21st century. *Annals of the American Academy for Political and Social Science* 522:104–115.

Dede, C., and D. Palumbo. 1990. Implications of hypermedia for cognition and communication. *Impact Assessment Bulletin* 9(1–2) (Summer, 1991):15–28.

Salzman, M., C. Dede, and B. Loftin. In press. Learner centered design of sensorily immersive microworlds using a virtual reality interface. Proceedings of the Seventh International Conference on Artificial Intelligence and Education. Charlottesville, VA: Association for the Advancement of Computers in Education.

Notes on Authors

Carmen Alvarez-Buylla is Directora Académica, Centro de Computo Académico at the Universidad Nacional Autonóma de México (UNAM). Address: Centro de Computo Académico, Circuito Exterior, Ciudad Universitaria UNAM, C.P. 04510, México D.F., México.

Christopher J. Dede is Professor of Information Technology and Education at George Mason University. Address: Graduate School of Education, George Mason University, 4400 University Drive, Fairfax, VA 22030.

Becky S. Duning is Senior Project Coordinator for the Western Joint Purchasing Initiative at the Western Interstate Commission for Higher Education (WICHE). Address: Western Interstate Commission for Higher Education, P.O. Drawer P, Boulder, CO 80301-9752.

Victor Guerra is Director General, Centro de Computo Académico at the Universidad Nacional Autonóma de México (UNAM). Address: Centro de Computo Académico, Circuito Exterior, Ciudad Universitaria UNAM, C.P. 04510, México D.F., México.

Shirley Hendrick is Associate Dean for Continuing and Distance Education at The Pennsylvania State University. Address: The Pennsylvania State University, 409 Business Adminstration, University Park, PA 16802.

Alejandro Mungaray is Academic Secretary at the National Association of Higher Education Institutions of Mexico (ANUIES). Address: National Association of Higher Education Institutions of Mexico, Tenayuca 200, Col Santa Cruz Atoyax, Mexico, D. F. CP. 03310, Mexico.

Stephen Murgatroyd is Professor and Executive Director of the Centre for Innovative Management at Athabasca University. Address: Athabasca University, St. Albert Centre, P.O. Box 65038, St. Albert, AB T8N 3Y5, Canada.

Von Pittman is Associate Dean of Continuing Education at The University of Iowa. Address: The University of Iowa, 116 International Center, Iowa City, IA 52242.

Judith M. Roberts is the Principal of Roberts and Associates/Associes. Address: Roberts and Associates/Associes, 20 Prince Arthur Avenue, Suite 9G, Toronto, ON M5R 1B1, Canada.

Linda L. Wolcott is Assistant Professor of Instructional Technology at Utah State University. Address: Utah State University, Department of Instructional Technology, Logan, UT 84322-2830.

This monograph was developed and produced by Margaret A. Koble with the assistance of Kathy J. Barrickman. Address: The Pennsylvania State University, The American Center for the Study of Distance Education, 403 South Allen Street, Suite 206, University Park, PA 16801-5202.

The American Journal of Distance Education

The American Journal of Distance Education is published by the American Center for the Study of Distance Education at The Pennsylvania State University. **The Journal** is designed for professional trainers; teachers in schools, colleges and universities; researchers; adult educators; and other specialists in education and communications. Created to disseminate information and act as a forum for criticism and debate about research in and the practice of distance education in the Americas, **The Journal** provides reports of new research, discussions of theory, and program developments in the field. **The Journal** is issued three times a year.

SELECTED CONTENTS

For information write to:
The American Journal of Distance Education
The Pennsylvania State University
403 South Allen Street, Suite 206
University Park, PA 16801-5202
Tel: (814) 863-3764   Fax: (814) 865-5878